Introduction

D1076814

AS this book goes to press the Royal Fleet Auxilia
mature age of 80 years. On 3 August 1905 instructions went out from the Admiralty that their auxiliary vessels should henceforth be known as "Royal Fleet Auxiliaries". Subsequently the Service was given its own flag —the Blue Ensign defaced in the fly by a vertical gold anchor. An Order-in-Council of 1911 firmly placed the RFA, within the area of commercial shipping by providing for its ships to be registered under the Merchant Shipping Acts. In 1985 however plans were announced to deregister the Fleet due to its increasing "front line" military role.

Today the Royal Fleet Auxiliary Service is operated by the Director of Supplies and Transport (Ships and Fuel) whose directorate forms part of the Royal Naval Supply and Transport Service (RNSTS) within the Ministry of Defence (Navy). In overall charge is the Director General of Supplies and Transport, a civil servant who, himself, reports to the Chief of Fleet Support, an Admiralty Board member.

All RFAs are manned by Merchant Navy personnel, which has the advantage of making their presence acceptable in neutral ports in time of war or where delicate international relations exist.

With fuel and stores supplied afloat by the RFA fleet, the Royal Navy no longer has to depend on overseas bases (which in any event are no longer available) and is given the facility of world-wide freedom of movement.

The seminal year of 1905 has been taken as the starting point of this book, in that only those RFAs built on or after that date have been included. A few anomalies unfortunately result in the cases of those vessels constructed prior to this but not taken up for RFA service until 1905. Details of those may be found in ROYAL FLEET AUXILIARY by Captain E S Sigwart (Adlard Coles 1969) which has been a valuable source of reference in the compilation of this book.

Pennant Numbers were not allocated to all ships but have been included when numbers were issued.

On 8th June 1982 the two RFA's *Sir Galahad* and *Sir Tristram* were landing troops ashore at Fitzroy during the Falklands Campaign. Television film of the horrific results of the Argentine bombing raid on the ships have been seen around the world.

RFA *Sir Tristram* has been rebuilt but her sister ship RFA *Sir Galahad* lies at the bottom of the South Atlantic Ocean. Her name, however, will live on. An appeal has been raised to commemorate the ship—and the 10 men of the RFA who lost their lives in the conflict.

The proceeds of the fund will help to purchase a new 'Tyne' class lifeboat which will be named 'RFA *Sir Galahad*' and will be based at Tenby in South Wales.

A proportion of the cover price of the book will be donated to the RFA Sir Galahad Lifeboat Appeal Fund.

Thank you for your support.

£4.95

The circular letter that started it all . . . .

CIRCULAR LETTER.

No. 9.

T. 3487.
1905.

ADMIRALTY, S.W.,

3rd August 1905.

MY Lords Commissioners of the Admiralty have decided that the title " H.M.S." shall in future be strictly confined to commissioned ships flying the white ensign and shall never be applied to fleet auxiliaries which are manned with mercantile crews, whether they are owned by the Admiralty or taken up on Transport charter.

My Lords are pleased therefore to direct that auxiliaries which belong to the Admiralty shall in future be styled "Royal Fleet Auxiliaries," and that those which are taken up on Transport charter shall be styled "Mercantile Fleet Auxiliaries."

The special character of any of these ships should be denoted after the name, and whenever brevity is desired the initials " R.F.A." or " M.F.A." for the two classes respectively should be used. Thus the "Maine" should be styled R.F.A. "Maine," Hospital Ship, and the "Sirdar," M.F.A. "Sirdar," Collier Transport.

By Command of their Lordships,

Evan Macgregor.

To all Commanders-in-Chief,
Captains, Commanders, and
Commanding Officers of
H.M. Ships and Vessels.

⟡ (3)38696.   1200.—8/05. P. 764. Wt 9638. E & S

Acknowledgements

The assistance of Lt Cdr's J. Lamb and B. Warlow RN with the text and Messrs Wright & Logan and S. Goodman for kindly making their photographic libraries available is much appreciated.

THE ROYAL FLEET AUXILIARY —

THE VITAL LINK

A Brief History

FLEET support is as old as the Royal Navy, which is generally considered to have become an entity in the reign of Henry VIII who built large armed ships to counter the maritime power of France and Spain.

Sometimes referred to as 'pinks', and were often redundant warships or prizes, these early supply vessels, deeply laden with provisions (including livestock), timber, canvas, cordage and a whole range of necessities would accompany the wide-ranging fleets of Grenville, Frobisher, Drake and other Tudor and Elizabethan admirals.

The squadron of six ships with which Anson set out in 1740 on the voyage that was to take him round the world, was accompanied by two victualling ships, *Anna* and *Industry.* And later, during the Seven Years' War and the War of American Independence, the Fleet in North American waters could never have been maintained without afloat support. Nor could Hawke have kept up his prolonged and arduous blockade of Brest which culminated in the great victory of Quiberon Bay in 1759: neither would Nelson have been able to fight his brilliant Mediterranean campaign 40 years later without stores and ammunitions brought to him from Gibraltar.

The growth of the Empire and the period of comparative peace from 1815 to 1914 meant that there were plenty of countries printed in red in the world atlas which could be used for replenishment of fuel and stores: at the same time, however, any reduction in the need for afloat support was outweighed by the conquest of steam over sail. Thus, despite the establishing of coaling stations in strategicaly situated ports, colliers were needed to serve the Navy's fleets and squadrons operating world-wide.

At the outset of World War I the Fleet was almost entirely coal burning: just four years later oil was the main fuel and during that time the Royal Fleet Auxiliary Service had expanded from a mere seven ships to as many as 85.

The Navy entered World War II reasonably well supported but operations with the United States Navy in the Pacific led to developments in support afloat which, in principle, are still with us, the "Fleet Train" was born. This is defined in the Oxford Companion to Ships and the Seas as '. . . the generic term used during the Second World War to describe an assembly of auxiliary vessels, such as oilers, repair ships, replenishment aircraft carriers, provision and store ships, etc, which accompanied the fighting fleet to sea on operations and enabled it to remain operational at sea for long periods without having to return to port to replenish. The term now usually employed for this function is afloat support.'

That definition broadly holds good today except, insofar as the Royal Navy is concerned, fleets are things of the past and one must now think in terms of flotillas, task forces and groups.

Methods and techniques of afloat support have developed greatly, not only due to experience with the Fleet Train but also resulting from the impetus given to replenishment at sea to satisfy the needs of thirsty

Atlantic convoy escorts. A decisive factor has been the virtual disappearance of overseas bases.

Thus the laborious and tricky astern procedure for replenishment at sea (RAS) familiar to, and unloved by, destroyer men has now been augmented by the abeam method by derrick and jackstay for fuel and stores, even three ships replenishing simultaneously. Vertical replenishment (VERTREP) is the latest technique whereby helicopters transfer stores by "netted" loads, and was much used in the Falklands War. As will be seen from the illustrations, virtually all RFAs now have flight decks; some ships carry a full range of supplies as well as fuel.

It is fair to say that the Falklands operation could not have been prosecuted without the support of RFAs and chartered merchant ships. In fact, it took more merchant than war ships to regain the islands!

As the shape of the Royal Navy of the next decade emerges, so does that of the RFA. 1985 sees the RFA fleet with more ships than planned had the 1981 Defence Review been implemented and the Falklands War not happened. The implications of both could produce a somewhat different RFA Service for the late 1980s than was originally envisaged.

RAS — The RFA's Olwen & Reliant keep station on the 'carrier Hermes as her tanks & store rooms are filled.

PART 1 — Tankers
The earliest ships . . . .

Ship	Completion Date	Builder	Propulsion
KHARKI	1899	Irvine Shipbuilding & Eng. Co. Ltd.	Steam

Displacement 675 tons gross   **Dimensions** 185 x 29 x 12ft   **Speed** 10 knots

Notes:
Same engines as "Mercedes" and "Petroleum" but built and fitted by McKie and Baxter Ltd. Purchased by the Admiralty in 1900. Originally built as a collier but converted to a tanker in 1906. Whilst based on the China Station in 1924 she was caught in a typhoon and badly damaged. Sold in 1931.

RFA Mercedes

Ship	Completion Date	Builder	Propulsion
MERCEDES	1901	Northumberland Shipping Co. Ltd. Howdon on Tyne	Steam

Displacement 4,487 tons gross 7,500 tons deadweight
Dimensions 351 x 51 x 28.5ft   **Speed** 12 knots

Notes:
Her steam single screw triple expansion engines were built and fitted by the North Eastern Marine and Eng. Co. Ltd. Purchased by the Admiralty in 1908 and used for coaling experiments. Sold in 1920 to Spanish owners. Foundered in 1936.

Ship	Completion Date	Builder	Propulsion
PETROLEUM	1903	Swan Hunters	Steam

Displacement 4,686 tons gross 6,100 tons deadweight
Dimensions 370.5 x 48.5 x 29.5ft   **Speed** 10.5 knots

Notes:
Engines were of the same type as "Mercedes". Originally fitted for oil burning. Purchased by the Admiralty in 1906. Her pumping equipment was so arranged that she could be towed behind battleships while refuelling. Spent most of her time at Scapa Flow. Sold for scrap in 1936 as part payment for HMS Majestic.

RFA Petroleum

Ship	Completion Date	Builder	Propulsion
NUCULA	1906	Armstrong Whitworth	Steam

Displacement 4614 GRT   **Dimensions** 370 x 48.5 28.5ft   **Speed** 10 knots

Notes:
Acquired by Admiralty in 1922 for China Station. Base oiler at Nagasaki during Yokohama relief operations 1923. Transferred to RNZN 1924. Fuelling hulk WW II.

Ship	Completion Date	Builder	Propulsion
ISLA	1903	Garston Graving Dock	Steam

Displacement 518 GRT   **Dimensions** 170 x 26 x 11ft   **Speed** 10 knots

Notes:
Purchased 1907 and used as first Admiralty spirit carrier, carrying light oil for submarines. Sold 1921.

Ship	Completion Date	Builder	Propulsion
DELPHINULA	1908	Armstrong Whitworth	Steam

Displacement 5238 GRT. 7100 tons deadweight   **Dimensions** 385 x 50 x 29ft
Speed 10 knots

Notes:
Acquired by Admiralty during WW I and used for oil freighting. From 1936 in use as oil hulk at Alexandria. Then Gibraltar. Sold in 1946 to Spanish breakers.

Ship	Completion Date	Builder	Propulsion
SANTA MARGHERITA	1916	Vickers	Diesel

Displacement 7513 GRT   **Dimensions** 440 x 54.5 x 36.5ft   **Speed** 11 knots

Notes:
A very advanced experimental ship. Designed by the Admiralty. Sold to Anglo Saxon Petroleum Co. 1920 and renamed "Marinula". Renamed "Trigonia" 1927. Was at Freetown 1939 as oil hulk; Gibraltar 1946. Scrapped 1950.

RFA Delphinula

First 2000 ton class

Ship	Completion Date	Builder	Propulsion
BURMA	1911	Greenock & Grangemouth Dockyard Co.	Steam

Displacement 1832 GRT 2500 tons deadweight
Dimensions 270.5 x 36.5 x 22ft   **Speed** 12 knots

Notes:
Designed to fuel battleships at sea while being towed or from alongside in harbour. Scrapped 1935 after spending 1926-35 in reserve at Rosyth.

Ship	Completion Date	Builder	Propulsion
MIXOL	1916	Caledon	Steam

Displacement 1977 GRT 2100 tons deadweight
Dimensions 270 x 38.5 x 23ft   **Speed** 12 knots

Notes:
Stability unsatisfactory and laid up at Gibraltar 1922-35. After WW II service, for which the top weight was reduced, she was sold to British commercial owners 1948.

RFA's Mixol & Thermol laid up at Gibraltar

RFA Thermol

Ship	Completion Date	Builder	Propulsion
THERMOL	1916	Greenock & Grangemouth Dockyard Co.	Steam

Displacement 1902 GRT 2000 tons deadweight
Dimensions 270 x 38.5 x 23ft   **Speed** 10.5 knots.

Notes:
Suffered same problems as "Mixol" and also kept in reserve in Gibraltar 1922-35. Top weight similarly reduced in 1940. Sold 1948.

Ship	Completion Date	Builder	Propulsion
TREFOIL	1917	Pembroke Dock but completed by Vickers	Diesel

Displacement 2070 GRT 2100 tons deadweight
Dimensions 279 x 39 x 22ft   **Speed** 12 knots

Notes:
Reserve at Rosyth 1923 until scrapped 1935.

Ship	Completion Date	Builder	Propulsion
TURMOIL	1917	Pembroke Dock	Steam

Displacement 2079 tons gross 2100 tons deadweight
Dimensions 279 x 39 x 22ft   **Speed** 12 knots

Notes:
Similar to "Trefoil" except steam propulsion. Rosyth 1923-35 then scrapped. Neither of these experimental sister ships was mechanically satisfactory and they saw little service.

World War I Construction Programme

Three classes were built for RFA service, the 1000 ton, 2000 ton and 5000 ton designs. Most of these ships remained in service until WW II.

First 1000 Ton Class

Ship	Completion Date	Builder	Propulsion
ATTENDANT	1914	Chatham Dockyard	Steam

Displacement 1016 tons gross 1025 tons deadweight
Dimensions 200 x 34 x 15ft   **Speed** 8 knots

Notes:
Employed mostly dockyard fuelling. In Reserve at Rosyth 1926-35, then sold but chartered back in WW II and based Scapa Flow.

CAROL	1914	Devonport Dockyard	Diesel

Displacement 1054 tons gross   **Dimensions** 200 x 34 x 15ft   **Speed** 8 knots

Notes:
Dockyard service, then Reserve at Rosyth 1926-35, then scrapped at Bo'ness.

FEROL	1914	Devonport Dockyard	Diesel

Displacement 1020 tons gross   **Dimensions** 200 x 34 x 15ft   **Speed** 8 knots

Notes:
Sold 1921 to British Owners. 1940 Bombed & sunk off Co. Wicklow.

SERVITOR	1915	Chatham Dockyard	Steam

Displacement 1023 tons gross   **Dimensions** 200 x 34 x 15ft   **Speed** 8 knots

Notes:
Sold 1922 after Dockyard Service at Sheerness.

Second 1000 Ton Class

Ship	Completion Date	Builder	Propulsion
CREOSOL	1916	Short	Steam

Displacement 1179 tons gross **Dimensions** 220 (O.A.) x 34.5 x 16.5ft
Speed 11-12 knots

Notes:
Torpedoed and sunk east coast 1918.

Ship	Completion Date	Builder	Propulsion
DISTOL	1916	Dobson	Steam

Displacement 1174 tons gross **Dimensions** 220 (O.A.) x 34.5 x 16.5ft
Speed 11-12 knots

Notes:
Was sold to Kuwait owners after Dockyard Service 1946.

Ship	Completion Date	Builder	Propulsion
KIMMEROL	1916	Craig Taylor	Steam

Displacement 1172 tons gross **Dimensions** 220 (O.A.) x 34.5 x 16.5ft
Speed 11-12 knots

Notes:
Was Dockyard manned until transferred to RFA in 1939. East Indies 1945-46.
Sold to British Owners 1947.

Ship	Completion Date	Builder	Propulsion
PHILOL	1916	Tyne Iron Shipbuilding	Steam

Displacement 1178 tons gross **Dimensions** 220 (O.A.) x 34.5 x 16.5ft
Speed 11-12 knots

Notes:
Ended her career as a tank hulk at Chatham in 1967 after life-long service as
port oiler round the UK.

Ship	Completion Date	Builder	Propulsion
SCOTOL	1916	Tyne Iron Shipbuilding	Steam

Displacement 1177 tons gross   **Dimensions** 220 (O.A.) x 34.5 x 16.5ft
Speed 11-12 knots

Notes:
Was port oiler at Dover. Then Portland until 1948 when she was sold to British Owners. In 1969 she was wrecked on Trevose Head while on passage to breakers. It transpired that her master thought he was off the Lizard on the opposite side of the Cornish Peninsula!

Ship	Completion Date	Builder	Propulsion
VISCOL	1916	Crais Taylor	Steam

Displacement 1163 tons gross   **Dimensions** 220 (O.A.) x 34.5 x 16.5ft
Speed 11-12 knots

Notes:
Was port oiler atGibraltar until sold to British Owners 1948.

Ship	Completion Date	Builder	Propulsion
BIRCHOL	1917	Barclay Curle	Steam

Displacement 1115 tons gross **Dimensions** 220 (O.A.) x 34.5 x 16.5ft
Speed 11-12 knots

Notes:
Saw Dockyard Service until 1939 when she was stranded and lost in the Hebrides.

RFA Boxol (1933)

Ship	Completion Date	Builder	Propulsion
BOXOL	1917	Barclay Curle	Steam

Displacement 1115 tons gross **Dimensions** 220 (O.A.) x 34.5 x 16.5ft
Speed 11-12 knots

Notes:
Stationed Malta 1921-48. Remarkably survived WW II unscathed and gave valuable service. Sold to Greece but re-acquired for Korean War and stationed at Gibraltar. Sold for scrap 1959-60.

Ship	Completion Date	Builder	Propulsion
EBONOL	1917	Clyde Shipbuilding	Steam

Displacement 1158 tons gross **Dimensions** 220 (O.A.) x 34.5 x 16.5ft
Speed 11-12 knots

Notes:
Her career began with Dockyard Service but she was sent to Hong Kong in 1931. Scuttled there December 1941 to avoid capture but raised by the Japanese and refitted. Recovered in Java (1945) then towed to, and sold at, Singapore. She sank off China coast 1950.

RFA Elderol

Ship	Completion Date	Builder	Propulsion
ELDEROL	1917	Swan Hunter	Steam

Displacement 1170 tons gross   **Dimensions** 220 (O.A.) x 34.5 x 16.5ft
Speed 11-12 knots

Notes:
Scrapped 1959 after UK Service.

Ship	Completion Date	Builder	Propulsion
ELMOL	1917	Swan Hunter	Steam

Displacement 1170 tons gross   **Dimensions** 220 (O.A.) x 34.5 x 16.5ft
Speed 11-12 knots

Notes:
Served in UK until chartered out in 1956. Sold to British Owners 1959.

Ship	Completion Date	Builder	Propulsion
LARCHOL	1917	Lobnitz	Steam

Displacement 1097 tons gross   **Dimensions** 220 (O.A.) x 34.5 x 16.5ft
Speed 11-12 knots

Notes:
Was at Sheerness and on East coast 1920-25. Scrapped 1958.

Ship	Completion Date	Builder	Propulsion
LIMOL	1917	Lobnitz	Steam

Displacement 1159 tons gross   **Dimensions** 220 (O.A.) x 34.5 x 16.5ft
Speed 11-12 knots

Notes:
Her service was entirely around home dockyards until scrapped in 1959.

RFA Limol (May 1952)

Ship	Completion Date	Builder	Propulsion
OAKOL	1918	Gray	Diesel

Displacement 1144 tons gross   **Dimensions** 220 (O.A.) x 34.5 x 16.5ft
Speed 11-12 knots

Notes:
Sold to British Owners 1920.

Ship	Completion Date	Builder	Propulsion
PALMOL	1918	Gray	Diesel

Displacement 1144 tons gross   **Dimensions** 220 (O.A.) x 34.5 x 16.5ft
Speed 11-12 knots

Notes:
Sold to British Owners 1920.

Ship	Completion Date	Builder	Propulsion
SPRUCOL	1918	Short	Diesel

Displacement 1137 tons gross   **Dimensions** 220 (O.A.) x 34.5 x 16.5ft
Speed 11-12 knots

Notes:
Sold to British Owners 1921.

Ship	Completion Date	Builder	Propulsion
TEAKOL (2)	1918	Short	Diesel

Displacement 1137 tons gross   **Dimensions** 220 (O.A.) x 34.5 x 16.5ft
Speed 11-12 knots

Notes:
Sold to British Owners 1921.

Ship	Completion Date	Builder	Propulsion
HICKOROL	1918	MacMillan	Steam

Displacement 1176 tons gross   **Dimensions** 220 (O.A.) x 34.5 x 16.5ft

Notes:
Was a Dockyard oiler 1920-32. Chartered out 1932-36. After war service she was sold to British Owners 1947.

Other vessels . . . .

RFA Ruthenia (1921)

Ship	Completion Date	Builder	Propulsion
RUTHENIA	1903	Barclay Curle	Steam

Displacement 7239 tons gross **Dimensions** 446 x 52 x 27.5ft
Speed 12.5 knots

Notes:
Sold to Admiralty 1914. Converted to dummy battleship (King George V) 1915. Converted to tanker for service at Scapa Flow. China station 1919-1927 then oil hulk at Singapore. Scuttled on Japanese invasion but refloated by invaders and used as a troopship (Choran Maru) recovered by RN 1945 and scrapped 1947.

Ship	Completion Date	Builder	Propulsion
PERTHSHIRE	1893	Hawthorn, Leslie & Co. Ltd	Steam

Displacement 5865 tons gross   **Dimensions** 420 x 54 x 29ft
Speed 12 knots

Notes:
After service on Australian trade, acquired in 1914 and converted into dummy battleship (Vanguard). In 1915 converted to tanker/stores ship for service at Scapa Flow. Post War service in Malta and Bosphorous and subsequently became Mediterranean fleet supply ship for refrigerated stores until sold to Italian breakers 1934.

Ship	Completion Date	Builder	Propulsion
KURUMBA	1917	Swan Hunter	Steam

Displacement 3978 tons gross 5102 tons deadweight
Dimensions 366 x 45.5 x 28ft   **Speed** 10 knots

Notes:
Built for Admiralty for Australian service and sold to Australian Government 1919. In Reserve Cockatoo 1923-40. Served at Manus 1945-6. Sold 1948 to Panama.

Second 2000 Ton Class

Ship	Completion Date	Builder	Propulsion
BELGOL	1917	Irvine Shipbuilding	Steam

Displacement 2468 tons gross   **Dimensions** 342.5 x 41.5 x 25.5ft
Speed 15 knots

Notes:
Served at length on China Station after being in home waters and the Mediterranean. Saw action on the Yangtse in the 1930's. Scrapped 1958.

Ship	Completion Date	Builder	Propulsion
CELEROL	1917	Short Bros	Steam

Displacement 2649 tons gross   **Dimensions** 342.5 x 41.5 x 25.5ft
Speed 15 knots

Notes:
Was attached to the Grand Fleet in WW I and also saw service in the Baltic. Rosyth 1926-35, then Bermuda. Pacific Fleet train 1945, then Hong Kong until scrapped 1958.

RFA Fortol (Jan 1949)

Ship	Completion Date	Builder	Propulsion
FORTOL	1917	McMillan	Steam

Displacement 2629 tons gross   **Dimensions** 342.5 x 41.5 x 25.5ft
Speed 15 knots

Notes:
Was in UK, Mediterranean and Chinese waters until 1935. Then at Suez and Aden. At Scapa Flow and Lerwick during latter part of WW II. At Rosyth until scrapped 1958.

Ship	Completion Date	Builder	Propulsion
FRANCOL	1917	Earle's Shipbuilding and Engineering	Steam

Displacement 2607 tons gross   **Dimensions** 342.5 x 41.5 x 25.5ft
Speed 15 knots

Notes:
On China Station from 1920. Sunk off Java 1942 and survivors became POW's.

Ship	Completion Date	Builder	Propulsion
MONTENOL	1917	WM Gray	Steam

Displacement 2646 tons gross   **Dimensions** 342.5 x 41.5 x 25.5ft
Speed 15 knots

Notes:
Operated on Fleet Attendance Duties in the Mediterranean 1921-35. Then she returned to Rosyth. Similar duties during Spanish and Abyssinian Wars. Torpedoed off W Coast of Africa 1942 and sunk by gunfire from HM Ships.

Ship	Completion Date	Builder	Propulsion
PRESTOL	1917	Napier & Miller	Steam

Displacement 2629 tons gross   **Dimensions** 342.5 x 41.5 x 25.5ft
Speed 15 knots

Notes:
Her principal service was with the Home Fleet, based on **Portsmouth**. Scrapped 1958.

RFA Montenol (Feb 1938)

Ship	Completion Date	Builder	Propulsion
RAPIDOL	1917	WM Gray	Steam

Displacement 2649 tons gross   **Dimensions** 342.5 x 41.5 x 25.5ft
Speed 15 knots

Notes:
Was in the East Indies 1925-7 and South Atlantic Station 1928-32. Abyssinian War 1935-6, Scapa Flow 1939-44. At Normandy Landings, then with Pacific Fleet Train. Sold Far East 1946.

Ship	Completion Date	Builder	Propulsion
SERBOL	1918	Caledon Shipbuilding and Engineering	Steam

Displacement 2649 tons gross   **Dimensions** 342.5 x 41.5 x 25.5ft
Speed 15 knots

Notes:
Mediterranean 1918-24, then West Indies until 1932. Malta 1935-6 followed by UK waters for eight years. Ceylon 1944, Hong Kong 1945. Finally home service until scrapped in 1958.

Ship	Completion Date	Builder	Propulsion
SLAVOL	1918	Greenock & Grangemouth Dockyard	Steam

Displacement 2623 tons gross   **Dimensions** 342.5 x 41.5 x 25.5ft
Speed 15 knots

Notes:
Was in Archangel 1918 and the Mediterranean 1919-21. Accompanied HMS "Repulse" on the Prince of Wale's Tour. East Indies 1927-39. Transferred to the Mediterranean during WW II and torpedoed (1942) while ferrying supplies to Tobruk.

Ship	Completion Date	Builder	Propulsion
VITOL	1918	Greenock & Grangemouth Dockyard	Steam

Displacement 2639   **Dimensions** 342.5 x 41.5 x 25.5ft
Speed 15 knots

Notes:
Was mined and sunk in Irish Sea 1918.

The First Leafs

These ships, taken up in WW I, were emergency war construction and purchases; some were ex-liners formerly converted to dummy battleships. None were retained as RFAs after the conclusion of hostilities.

Ship	Completion Date	Builder	Propulsion
ASPENLEAF	1900	Barclay Curle	Steam

Displacement 6124 tons gross   **Dimensions** 446 x 52ft   **Speed** 13 knots

Notes:
Built for Elder Dempster line (Lake Eire). 1914 converted to dummy battleship (King George Class) subsequently served as tanker "Saxol". Scrapped 1925.

Ship	Completion Date	Builder	Propulsion
MAPLELEAF	1898	Swan Hunter & Wigham Richardson Ltd	Steam

Displacement 7998 tons gross   **Dimensions** 470 x 56ft   **Speed** 13 knots

Notes:
Built for Elder Dempster as liner "Mount Royal". Converted to dummy battleship (Marlborough), then as tanker "Rangol" until renamed. Sold 1919 to UK owners.

Ship	Completion Date	Builder	Propulsion
VINELEAF	1901	Swan Hunter & Wigham Richardson Ltd	Steam

Displacement 7678 tons gross   **Dimensions** 470 x 56ft   **Speed** 13 knots

Notes:
Built as Harrison liner "Patrician". 1914 converted to dummy battle cruiser (Invincible), then as tanker "Teakol" until renamed. Sold 1919 to UK Owners.

Ship	Completion Date	Builder	Propulsion
BAYLEAF	1894	Harland & Wolff	Steam

Displacement 8455 tons gross   **Dimensions** 500 x 60ft   **Speed** 13 knots

Notes:
Built at Belfast as White Star liner "Cevic". After service as dummy battle-cruiser (Queen Mary), converted to tanker "Bayol". Sold 1919 to UK Owners.

Ship	Completion Date	Builder	Propulsion
OAKLEAF	1899	A Stephens & Sons Ltd	Steam

Displacement 7345 tons gross   **Dimensions** 485 x 59ft   **Speed** 13 knots

Notes:
Built at Glasgow as Elder Dempster liner "Montezuma". Converted to dummy battleship (Iron Duke) 1914, then to a tanker "Abadol". Torpedoed 25th July, 1917.

Ship	Completion Date	Builder	Propulsion
ASHLEAF	1916	Ropner	Steam

Displacement 5768 tons gross   **Dimensions** 405 x 54 x 26ft
Speed 14 knots

Notes:
Ex "Olga". Sunk by torpedo SW appraoches 1916.

Ship	Completion Date	Builder	Propulsion
BIRCHLEAF	1916	Short	Steam

Displacement 5882 tons gross   **Dimensions** 405 x 54 x 26ft
Speed 14 knots

Notes:
Ex 'Oldbury'. Sold to British Owners.

Ship	Completion Date	Builder	Propulsion
BOXLEAF	1916	Barclay Curle	Steam

Displacement 7338 tons gross   **Dimensions** 450 x 58 x 26ft
Speed 14 knots.

Notes:
Originally a cargo ship. Ex 'Olinda". Sold 1919 to Dutch Owners.

Ship	Completion Date	Builder	Propulsion
BRIARLEAF	1916	Readhead, Southshields	Steam

Displacement 5882 tons gross   **Dimensions** 405 x 54 x 26ft
Speed 14 knots

Notes:
Ex "Oletta". Sold 1919 to British Owners.

Ship	Completion Date	Builder	Propulsion
LAURELEAF	1916	Craig Taylor	Steam

Displacement 5631 tons gross   **Dimensions** 405 x 54 x 26ft
Speed 14 knots

Notes:
Ex "Olalla". Sold to British Owners 1919.

Ship	Completion Date	Builder	Propulsion
LIMELEAF	1916	Barclay Curle	Steam

Displacement 7339 tons gross   **Dimensions** 450 x 58 x 26ft
Speed 14 knots

Notes:
Ex "Oligarch". Built as a cargo ship but converted. Conversion unsatisfactory & sold to Dutch Owners 1919.

Ship	Completion Date	Builder	Propulsion
PALMLEAF	1916	Irvine's Shipbuilding	Steam

Displacement 5489 tons gross   **Dimensions** 405 x 54 x 26ft
Speed 14 knots

Notes:
Ex "Oliphant". Sunk by submarine in western approaches 1917.

Ship	Completion Date	Builder	Propulsion
ROSELEAF	1916	Raylton Dixon	Steam

Displacement 6572 tons gross   **Dimensions** 418 x 54 x 26ft
Speed 14 knots

Notes:
Ex "Califol". Sold to UK Owners 1920.

Ship	Completion Date	Builder	Propulsion
BEECHLEAF	1917	Richardson, Duck & Co Ltd	Steam

Displacement 5861 tons gross   **Dimensions** 405 x 54 x 26ft
Speed 14 knots

Notes:
Ex "Olnos". Sold to British Owners 1919.

Ship	Completion Date	Builder	Propulsion
DOCKLEAF	1917	Bartram	Steam

Displacement 5311 tons gross   **Dimensions** 405 x 54 x 26ft
Speed 14 knots

Notes:
Ex 'Oleary'. Sold to British Owners 1919.

RFA Beechleaf

Ship	Completion Date	Builder	Propulsion
ELMLEAF	1917	Earle's Shipbuilding	Steam

Displacement 5948 tons gross **Dimensions** 405 x 54 x 26ft
Speed 14 knots

Notes:
Ex "Olivet". Sold to UK Owners 1919.

Ship	Completion Date	Builder	Propulsion
FERNLEAF	1917	Napier & Miller	Steam

Displacement 5938 tons gross **Dimensions** 405 x 54 x 26ft
Speed 14 knots

Notes:
Ex "Oleander". Sold to UK owners 1919.

Ship	Completion Date	Builder	Propulsion
HOLLYLEAF	1917	WM Hamilton	Steam

Displacement 5162 tons gross **Dimensions** 405 x 54 x 26ft
Speed 14 knots

Notes:
Ex "Oleaster". Sold to UK Owners 1919.

RFA Dredgol at Malta

Ship	Completion Date	Builder	Propulsion
DREDGOL	1918	Simons	Steam

Displacement 4000 tons gross   **Dimensions** 326 x 54.5 x 21.5ft
Speed 11 knots

Notes:
Built by Simons as a Calcutter dredger! Acquired by Admiralty, converted to tanker and sent to Hong Kong. Malta 1920-31. Scrapped 1935.

The 5000 Ton "Leaf" Class

Fast (for their day), good-looking ships, designed to act as escorts to Atlantic convoys while carrying oil from the USA to the UK. Unfortunately their fuel consumption was excessive. Originally their names were prefixed with "Ol" but this was changed to "Leaf" to conform with other Admiralty contract tankers.

RFA's Cherryleaf (R) & Brambleleaf at Malta (1934)

Ship	Completion Date	Builder	Propulsion
APPLELEAF	1917	Workman Clark	Steam

Displacement 5891 tons gross   **Dimensions** 425 x 54.5 x 25.5ft
Speed 16 knots

Notes:
Ex "Texol". Served in North Atlantic 1917-18 then to Mediterranean. Rosyth 1922-26. Chartered out until 1930. Freighting to West Indies 1930-33. To Hong Kong 1935 and in the Middle and Far East during WW II. Home waters from 1945 until scrapped in 1946.

Ship	Completion Date	Builder	Propulsion
BRAMBLELEAF	1917	Russell	Steam

Displacement 5912 tons gross **Dimensions** 425 x 54.5 x 25.5ft
Speed 16 knots

Notes:
Ex "Rumol". Was in the Dardanelles 1919-22 after WW I North Atlantic service, then Gibraltar until 1925. Subsequently acted as Fleet Attendant Mediterranean and was torpedoed 1942 between Alexandria and Tobruk. Towed to Alexandria where she became an oil hulk. Scrapped 1947.

Ship	Completion Date	Builder	Propulsion
CHERRYLEAF	1917	Dixon	Steam

Displacement 5896 tons gross **Dimensions** 425 x 54.5 x 25.5ft
Speed 16 knots

Notes:
Ex "Persol". Had similar North Atlantic Service as "Brambleleaf" and was later in Bermuda. Rosyth 1922-26. Then on Charter until 1931. Mediterranean station until 1945 followed by East Indies. Fitted with camouflage plates on her funnel — to make it look upright.

Ship	Completion Date	Builder	Propulsion
ORANGELEAF	1917	Thomson	Steam

Displacement 5927 tons gross **Dimensions** 425 x 54.5 x 25.5ft
Speed 16 knots

Notes:
Ex "Bornol". After convoy escort duties she was at Rosyth (Reserve) 1922-26. On charter until 1932 then at Bermuda. West coast South America 1939-40. Finally to the Eastern Fleet via UK. Scrapped 1946.

Ship	Completion Date	Builder	Propulsion
PEARLEAF	1917	Gray	Steam

Displacement 5911 tons gross **Dimensions** 425 x 54.5 x 25.5ft
Speed 16 knots

Notes:
Ex "Gypol". After convoy escort duties, joined her sisters in Reserve at Rosyth 1922-26. Chartered out until 1930, then Admiralty freighting. China station and Far East during WW II. Scrapped 1946.

Ship	Completion Date	Builder	Propulsion
PLUMLEAF	1917	Swan Hunter & Wigham Richardson	Steam

Displacement 5916 tons gross **Dimensions** 425 x 54.5 x 25.5ft
Speed 16 knots

Notes:
Ex "Trinol". Her early career was similar to the previous four. Mediterranean station until bombed and sunk Malta 1942. Raised and scrapped 1947.

RFA Cherryleaf (Aug 1930)

Spirit Carriers — Pet Class

RFA Petrobus

Ship	Completion Date	Builder	Propulsion
PETRELLA	1918	Dunlop Bremner	Steam

Displacement 475 tons gross **Dimensions** 155 x 28 x 11ft
Speed 11 knots

Notes:
Sold 1946 after UK service.

Ship	Completion Date	Builder	Propulsion
PETROBUS	1918	Dunlop Bremner	Steam

Displacement 475 tons gross **Dimensions** 155 x 28 x 11ft
Speed 11 knots

Notes:
UK service then scrapped 1959.

Ship	Completion Date	Builder	Propulsion
PETRONEL	1918	Dunlop Bremner	Steam

Displacement 475 tons gross **Dimensions** 155 x 28 x 11ft
Speed 11 knots

Notes:
Converted to water carrier for service with Atlantic Fleet. Sold UK 1945.

Sprite Class

RFA Nasprite — Note the car on board!

Ship	Completion Date	Builder	Propulsion
NASPRITE (A252)	1941	Blythswood Shipbuilding	Steam

Displacement 965 tons gross   **Dimensions** 204 x 33 x 13.5ft
Speed 10 knots

Notes:
UK and Mediterranean service. Scrapped 1964.

AIRSPRITE	1941	Blythswood Shipbuilding	Steam

Displacement 970 tons gross   **Dimensions** 204 x 33 x 13.5ft
Speed 10 knots

Notes:
Scrapped 1965 after similar service.

War Class — First Series

Standard WW I cargo ship, oil burning. Carried over 7000 tons oil plus naval stores if necessary. The first six of the class each had five cargo tanks. The second nine had 7 cargo tanks each.

Ship	Completion Date	Builder	Propulsion
WAR BAHADUR	1918	Armstrong Whitworth	Steam

Displacement 5565 tons gross **Dimensions** 410 x 52.5 x 28ft
Speed 10 knots

Notes:
Stationed Rosyth 1931-35. After severe heavy weather damage in 1939 she became a fuelling hulk at Devonport until scrapped in 1947.

Ship	Completion Date	Builder	Propulsion
WAR NIZAM	1918	Palmer	Steam

Displacement 5592 tons gross **Dimensions** 410 x 52.5 x 28ft
Speed 10 knots

Notes:
Saw action with East coast convoys before becoming a fuelling hulk. Scrapped 1949.

RFA War Diwan (1932)

Ship	Completion Date	Builder	Propulsion
WAR DIWAN	1919	Lithgow	Steam

Displacement 5551 tons gross **Dimensions** 410 x 52.5 x 28ft
Speed 10 knots

Notes:
Was mined and sunk in River Scheldt 1944.

Ship	Completion Date	Builder	Propulsion
WAR NAWAB	1919	Palmer	Steam

Displacement 5577 tons gross **Dimensions** 410 x 52.5 x 28ft
Speed 10 knots

Notes:
Her service was in home waters, finally as an oil hulk at Devonport from 1939. Scrapped 1958.

Ship	Completion Date	Builder	Propulsion
WAR PATHAN	1919	Laing	Steam

Displacement 5581 tons gross **Dimensions** 410 x 52.5 x 28ft
Speed 10 knots

Notes:
Sold UK 1947.

Ship	Completion Date	Builder	Propulsion
WAR SEPOY	1919	Gray	Steam

Displacement 5557 tons gross **Dimensions** 410 x 52.5 x 28ft
Speed 10 knots

Notes:
Took first load of oil to the new Admiralty tanks at Singapore in 1922. Transferred to Director of Stores 1937. Bombed at Dover while fuelling the Dunkirk "Fleet" in 1940 and was later sunk there as a blockship.

Second Series

Ship	Completion Date	Builder	Propulsion
WAR KRISHNA	1919	Swan Hunter & Wigham Richardson	Steam

Displacement 5730 tons gross   **Dimensions** 410 x 52.5 x 28ft
Speed 10 knots

Notes:
She was the only ship of class with funnel and engines aft. Sold 1947 to Indian Owners.

Ship	Completion Date	Builder	Propulsion
WAR HINDOO	1919	Hamilton	Steam

Displacement 5565 tons gross   **Dimensions** 410 x 52.5 x 28ft
Speed 10 knots

Notes:
After WW II service as harbour oiler at Milford Haven sailed to Singapore and Hong Kong. Fuelling hulk at Malta from 1949 until scrapped 1958.

Ship	Completion Date	Builder	Propulsion
WAR AFRIDI	1920	Duncan	Steam

Displacement 5561 tons gross   **Dimensions** 410 x 52.5 x 28ft
Speed 10 knots

Notes:
Normal RFA service. Storage hulk at Hong Kong Post WW II. Scrapped 1950.

Ship	Completion Date	Builder	Propulsion
WAR BHARATA	1920	Palmer	Steam

Displacement 5600 tons gross   **Dimensions** 410 x 52.5 x 28ft
Speed 10 knots

Notes:
Saw normal RFA service and sold in UK 1948.

RFA War Afridi (March 1931)

Ship	Completion Date	Builder	Propulsion
WAR BRAHMIN	1920	Lithgow	Steam

Displacement 5545 tons gross   **Dimensions** 410 x 52.5 x 28ft
Speed 10 knots

Notes:
Following varied RFA duties she was a water carrier in the Mediterranean and used for oil storage at Gibraltar until scrapped in 1960.

Ship	Completion Date	Builder	Propulsion
WAR MEHTAR	1920	Armstrong Whitworth	Steam

Displacement 5502 tons gross   **Dimensions** 410 x 52.5 x 28ft
Speed 10 knots

Notes:
Became RFA in 1926, then chartered out for two years; sunk by a U-boat near Harwich 1941.

Ship	Completion Date	Builder	Propulsion
WAR PINDARI	1920	Lithgow	Steam

Displacement 5548 tons gross   **Dimensions** 410 x 52.5 x 28ft
Speed 10 knots

Notes:
Sold to British Owners in 1948 after normal RFA service.

Ship	Completion Date	Builder	Propulsion
WAR SIRDAR	1920	Laing	Steam

Displacement 5518 tons gross   **Dimensions** 410 x 52.5 x 28ft
Speed 10 knots

Notes:
In 1942 Bombed and stranded in Sunda Straits. Salvaged by Japanese (renamed Honan Maru) and sunk by US Submarine 1945.

Ship	Completion Date	Builder	Propulsion
WAR SUDRA	1920	Palmer	Steam

Displacement 5599 tons gross   **Dimensions** 410 x 52.5 x 28ft
Speed 10 knots

Notes:
Spent WW II in Iceland and at Scapa Flow and finally at Hong Kong as floating storage. Sold to British Owners 1948.

This photo taken at Malta in Nov 1928 shows Admiralty tugs manoeuvring the heavily laden "War Brahmin" as she arrives from Sicily with fresh water. On account of cholera precautions, ships passing through Egyptian ports called at Malta for drinking water. As Malta's water supply was unable to cope with the demand—the water was brought from Sicily by the RFA.

The "OI" Class

Ship	Completion Date	Builder	Propulsion
OLCADES	1918	Workman Clark	Steam

Displacement 6891 tons gross **Dimensions** 443.5 x 57 x 33ft
Speed 10 knots

Notes:
Was chartered out until 1936 then used to replenish naval storage tanks overseas. Oil hulk at Bombay 1942 for a year until sent to join Eastern Fleet. At Singapore 1946-53, then scrapped UK.

Ship	Completion Date	Builder	Propulsion
OLIGARCH	1918	Workman Clark	Steam

Displacement 6897 tons gross **Dimensions** 443.5 x 57 x 33ft
Speed 10 knots

Notes:
After similar peace time service to "Olcades", she was on Russian convoys in 1944 disguised as a cargo ship with a funnel amidships. Torpedoed in Eastern Mediterranean 1943 but survived and stationed at Alexandria as a fuel hulk. Scuttled in Red Sea 1946 loaded with obsolete ammunition.

RFA Oligarch sails (29 May 1943) from South Shields. Note dummy funnel amidships.

RFA Olynthus (Aug 1939)

Ship	Completion Date	Builder	Propulsion
OLYNTHUS	1918	Swan Hunter & Wigham	Steam

Displacement 6688 tons gross   **Dimensions** 443.5 x 57 x 33ft
Speed 10 knots

Notes:
Began her career like the others. In 1940, she was attached to the Squadron hunting the Graf Spee and, after fuelling them at sea, saw the battle. Escort oiler 1941, Eastern fleet 1942-45. Sold to Italian Owners 1947.

Ship	Completion Date	Builder	Propulsion
OLWEN	1917	Palmers Shipbuilding & Iron Co	Steam

Displacement 6470 tons gross   **Dimensions** 443.5 x 57 x 33ft
Speed 10 knots

Notes:
RFA manned from 1936 for fleet fuelling duties; Eastern fleet 1942-46. Sold to Pakistani Owners 1948.

Ship	Completion Date	Builder	Propulsion
OLNA	1921	Devonport Dockyard	Steam

Displacement 7023 tons gross   **Dimensions** 443.5 x 57 x 33ft
Speed 10 knots

Notes:
Was mostly on charter work until 1936. In 1939 she was severely damaged by stranding off Ceylon but repaired at Bombay. Bombed and sunk at Crete 1941.

Ship	Completion Date	Builder	Propulsion
OLEANDER	1922	Pembroke Dockyard	Steam

Displacement 7045 tons gross   **Dimensions** 443.5 x 57 x 33ft
Speed 10 knots

Notes:
In 1940 she was bombed and beached at Harstad, Norway.

RFA Olna (July 1930)

The "Dale" Class

FIRST GROUP

These six vessels entered RFA service in 1937, when the Admiralty decided it needed its own fleet of tankers. They were purchased off the slipway. Two more were acquired just before the outbreak of WW II and 10 more were taken up in 1941.

Ship	Completion Date	Builder	Propulsion
ABBEYDALE	1937	Swan Hunter & Wigham Richardson	Diesel

Displacement 8402 tons gross   **Dimensions** 483 x 62 x 34ft
Speed 11.5 knots

Notes:

Was torpedoed in the Mediterranean 1944. She broke in two and one half was towed to Bizerta, and later to Taranto, the other direct to Taranto where they were reunited. The result was a ship shorter by some 68ft. She was scrapped 1960.

Ship	Completion Date	Builder	Propulsion
ALDERSDALE	1937	Camell Laird	Diesel

Displacement 8402 tons gross   **Dimensions** 483 x 62 x 34ft
Speed 11.5 knots

Notes:

Assigned to the notorious Russian convoys in 1942. She was bombed and immobilised in the Barents Sea. The entire crew was transferred to HMS "Salamander" which attempted, unsuccessfully, to sink her. A U-boat succeeded in this later.

RFA Arndale (Apr 1952)

Ship	Completion Date	Builder	Propulsion
ARNDALE	1937	Swan Hunter & Wigham Richardson	Diesel

Displacement 8296 tons gross   **Dimensions** 483 x 62 x 34ft
Speed 11.5 knots

Notes:
With Pacific fleet in operations against Okinawa 1944-45. Scrapped 1960.

Ship	Completion Date	Builder	Propulsion
BISHOPDALE (A128)	1937	Lithgows	Diesel

Displacement 8406 tons gross   **Dimensions** 483 x 62 x 34ft
Speed 11.5 knots

Notes:
Served mostly in the Pacific and was particularly well armed for self protection. Hit by a Kamikaze bomber but (just) survived. Scrapped 1970.

RFA Bishopdale (Nov 1950)

Ship	Completion Date	Builder	Propulsion
BOARDALE	1937	Harland & Wolff	Diesel

Displacement 8334 tons gross   **Dimensions** 483 x 62 x 34ft
Speed 11.5 knots

Notes:
Struck a reef and sank at Narvik during Norwegian campaign (1940). Crew survived.

Ship	Completion Date	Builder	Propulsion
BROOMDALE	1937	Harland & Wolff	Diesel

Displacement 8334 tons gross   **Dimensions** 483 x 62 x 34ft
Speed 11.5 knots

Notes:
After service in the Norwegian campaign she was accidentally torpedoed by British submarine at Trincomalee in 1944. First RFA to be fitted with gantry king posts for RAS and also first to be provided with tank heating coils.

RFA Broomdale (Oct 1954)

SECOND GROUP

Purchased by the Admiralty from Shell Tanker Co. (while building) for evaluation purposes and comparison with its earlier purchases.

Ship	Completion Date	Builder	Propulsion
CAIRNDALE	1939	Harland & Wolff	Diesel

Displacement 8129 tons gross   **Dimensions** 483 x 59.5 x 34ft
Speed 11.5 knots

Notes:
Was sunk by Submarine in Eastern Atlantic 1941 while attached to Force H.

Ship	Completion Date	Builder	Propulsion
CEDARDALE	1939	Blythswood Shipbuilding	Diesel

Displacement 8132 tons gross   **Dimensions** 483 x 59.5 x 34ft
Speed 11.5 knots

Notes:
Survived the war after service in the Atlantic, Far East and Pacific, including Okinawa. Scrapped 1960.

THIRD GROUP: War Construction Programme

As WW II progressed, the Admiralty realised it would have to increase its tanker fleet and took over a number of vessels originally completed for the Eagle Oil Co. They were basically similar to the second (trial) group.

Ship	Completion Date	Builder	Propulsion
DARKDALE	1941	Blythswood Shipbuilding	Diesel

Displacement 8145 tons gross   **Dimensions** 483 x 59.5 x 34ft
Speed 11.5 knots

Notes:
Served as escort oiler on Atlantic convoys and fleet oiler South Africa. Torpedoed and sunk off St Helena 1941.

Ship	Completion Date	Builder	Propulsion
DENBYDALE	1941	Blythswood Shipbuilding	Diesel

Displacement 8145 tons gross   **Dimensions** 483 x 59.5 x 34ft
Speed 11.5 knots

Notes:
After duty as an escort oiler was stationed at Gibraltar where she was severely damaged by Italian frogmen 20 Sept 1941. She remained there as a fuel and accommodation hulk until scrapped 1957.

Ship	Completion Date	Builder	Propulsion
DERWENTDALE	1941	Harland & Wolff	Diesel

Displacement 8398 tons gross   **Dimensions** 483 x 59.5 x 34ft
Speed 11.5 knots

Notes:
Was completed as a landing ship gantry (LSG) and took part in landings on Madagascar, North Africa, Sicily and Italy. Survived 15 dive-bomb attacks on one single day but had to be towed to Malta—thence UK, where she received "Denbydale's" engines. In 1946, converted back to oiler and employed on Trinidad freighting run. Sold to Canadian Owners 1959.

Ship	Completion Date	Builder	Propulsion
DEWDALE	1941	Cammell Laird	Diesel

Displacement 8265 tons gross **Dimensions** 483 x 59.5 x 34ft
Speed 11.5 knots

Notes:
Completed as LSG. Survived heavy bombing during North African Landings off Bougie and shot down two JU88's and one torpedo bomber. Hit later at Algiers and returned to UK 1944. Later sent East and present at Malaya landings. Re-converted to tanker 1946-47 and employed freighting. Scrapped 1959.

Ship	Completion Date	Builder	Propulsion
DINGLEDALE	1941	Harland & Wolff	Diesel

Displacement 8145 tons gross **Dimensions** 483 x 59.5 x 34ft
Speed 11.5 knots

Notes:
Acted as escort oiler on Malta convoys and survived heavy bombing off Bone. Later with Pacific fleet train. Probably carried out first abeam RAS of a Battleship when she fuelled HMS King George V simultaneously with HM ships "Illustrious", "Black Prince" and "Wild Swan". Sold to Somali Owners 1959.

RFA Dingledale

Ship	Completion Date	Builder	Propulsion
ENNERDALE	1941	Swan Hunter & Wigham	Steam

Displacement 8150 tons gross   **Dimensions** 483 x 59.5 x 34ft
Speed 11.5 knots

Notes:
Completed as LSG and took part in the North Africa, Italian and Far East campaigns. Mined at Port Swettenham 1945 but reached Singapore although part of bottom blown away. Scrapped 1959.

RFA Ennerdale

ECHODALE	1941	Hawthorn Leslie	Diesel

Displacement 8150 tons gross   **Dimensions** 483 x 59.5 x 34ft
Speed 11.5 knots

Notes:
Eastern Fleet including Burma landings then peace time freighting. Scrapped 1961.

DINSDALE	1942	Harland & Wolff	Diesel

Displacement 8254 tons gross   **Dimensions** 483 x 59.5 x 34ft
Speed 11.5 knots

Notes:
Her career was short: she was sunk by submarine in the South Atlantic on her maiden voyage.

RFA Ennerdale as converted to Landing Ship (Gantry)

RFA Eaglesdale (May 1954)

Ship	Completion Date	Builder	Propulsion
EAGLESDALE	1942	Furness Shipbuilding	Steam

Displacement 8030 tons gross   **Dimensions** 483 x 59.5 x 34ft
Speed 11.5 knots

Notes:
Was used for trials of equipment following capture of German supply ship, including fitting of rubber hose and deck rollers. Subsequently with Eastern Fleet and on the South Atlantic station. Scrapped in Germany 1959.

Ship	Completion Date	Builder	Propulsion
EASEDALE	**1942**	**Furness Shipbuilding**	**Steam**

Displacement 8032 tons gross   **Dimensions** 483 x 59.5 x 34ft
Speed 11.5 knots

Notes:
With Eastern and Pacific fleets took part in landings against Madagascar and Sumatra. Scrapped 1960 after period in Reserve at Portland.

Note: Post-War "Dales" listed later in historical order.

The "Ranger" Class

They were replacements for the third group of "Dales" and the first tankers built after WW I specifically for the Admiralty: The "Rangers" became so adept at RAS that they could fuel three ships simultaneously.

Ship	Completion Date	Builder	Propulsion
BLACK RANGER (A163)	1940	Harland & Wolff	Diesel

Displacement 3313 tons gross   **Dimensions** 366 x 47 x 22.5ft
Speed 14 knots

Notes:
After War Service with Russian convoys she was stationed at Portland, also attached Training Squadron and Fishery Protection Squadron in the Arctic. Sold to Greek Owners 1973.

Ship	Completion Date	Builder	Propulsion
BLUE RANGER (A157)	1940	Harland & Wolff	Diesel

Displacement 3417 tons gross   **Dimensions** 366 x 47 x 22.5ft
Speed 14 knots

Notes:
Mainly based at Malta throughout her service. Sold in 1971.

Ship	Completion Date	Builder	Propulsion
BROWN RANGER (A169)	1940	Harland & Wolff	Diesel

Displacement 3417 tons gross   **Dimensions** 366 x 47 x 22.5ft
Speed 14 knots

Notes:
Mediterranean convoys and North Africa landings, then with British Pacific fleet for reoccupation of Singapore and Hong Kong. Scrapped 1975.

RFA Black Ranger

Ship	Completion Date	Builder	Propulsion
GOLD RANGER (A130)	1941	Caledon Shipbuilding	Diesel

Displacement 3313 tons gross   **Dimensions** 356 x 47 x 22.5ft
Speed 12 knots

Notes:
Was built 10ft shorter than rest of class and two knots slower. After War Service she was in Korean War and in support of atomic test at Muaro Atoll. She later was employed as a support ship for Minesweepers during Indonesian confrontation. Sold to Singapore Owners 1973.

GREY RANGER	1941	Caledon	Diesel

Displacement 3313 tons gross   **Dimensions** 356 x 47 x 22.5ft
Speed 12 knots

Notes:
Was similar in size and speed to "Gold Ranger". Fitted with the first successful self-tensioning winch for replenishment at sea. Torpedoed on convoy QP14 on 22nd September 1942, her engines wrecked, she was later sunk by HM ships in the area.

GREEN RANGER	1941	Caledon	Diesel

Displacement 3313 tons gross   **Dimensions** 356 x 47 x 22.5ft
Speed 12 knots

Notes:
Was similar in size and speed to "Gold Ranger". Originally, was the Navy's first large spirit carrier. She saw initial service in Canadian waters then sent east. Later in reserve at Plymouth and finally lost by stranding near Hartland, North Devon, whilst being towed to Cardiff for refit in 1962.

RFA Green Ranger

The "Wave" Class

During WW II there was a requirement for fast tankers to bring oil into the country but, by the time materials and shipyards were available, hostilities were almost over. They were offered to the Admiralty, who wanted faster tankers for the Pacific Fleet, and the class name was changed from "Empire" to "Wave". Twenty-one were built, of which the RFA took all but one, and their propulsion was changed from diesel to steam. They were not very satisfactory ships, but experience with them was embodied in the "Tide" class. The following were modified to fast fleet replenishment ships:-

Ship	Completion Date	Builder	Propulsion
WAVE VICTOR	1943	Furness Shipbuilding	Steam

Displacement 8128 tons gross **Dimensions** 494 x 64 x 35.5ft
Speed 13-15 knots

Notes:
Initially chartered out, as most were, she was nearly lost by fire off Lundy Island 1954. Involved in fisheries dispute with Iceland 1958-60, then was a fuel hulk at Gan for 10 years under Air Ministry ownership. Scrapped 1971.

RFA Wave Victor (Oct 1953)

Ship	Completion Date	Builder	Propulsion
WAVE MASTER (A193)	1944	Laing	Steam

Displacement 8199 tons gross   **Dimensions** 494 x 64 x 35.5ft
Speed 13-15 knots

Notes:
Was chartered out for first two years. Saw service during fisheries dispute 1958-61. Scrapped 1963-4.

Ship	Completion Date	Builder	Propulsion
WAVE KNIGHT (A249)	1945	Laing	Steam

Displacement 8187 tons gross   **Dimensions** 494 x 64 x 35.5ft
Speed 13-15 knots

Notes:
In 1962 she performed a notable feat when ordered to meet the freighting oiler "Orangeleaf" in the North Atlantic and take on more than 8000 tons of fuel required for a NATO exercise. This task was achieved, despite severe weather, overnight in 18 hours, and "Wave Knight" went on to RAS 55 ships of various nationalities during the next 16 days. Scrapped 1964-5.

Ship	Completion Date	Builder	Propulsion
WAVE PRINCE (A207)	1945	Laing	Steam

Displacement 8175 tons gross   **Dimensions** 494 x 64 x 35.5ft
Speed 13-15 knots

Notes:
Was at first on charter, then involved in fisheries dispute 1958-61. Acted as escort oiler for RoyalYacht on several occasions, including a visit by the Queen to Australia. She was at the Christmas Islands during H-Bomb tests. Sold 1971 for scrap.

Ship	Completion Date	Builder	Propulsion
WAVE SOVEREIGN (A211)	1945	Furness Shipbuilding	Steam

Displacement 8122 tons gross   **Dimensions** 494 x 64 x 35.5ft
Speed 13-15 knots

Notes:
A support ship during the Christmas Islands H-Bomb test, and in the 1958-61 fisheries dispute. Scrapped 1966.

The ships company "cheer ship" onboard RFA Wave Prince having supported the Royal Yacht on the Royal Tour of Australia/New Zealand (1962).

Ship	Completion Date	Builder	Propulsion
WAVE BARON (A242)	1946	Furness Shipbuilding	Steam

Displacement 8174 tons gross   **Dimensions** 494 x 64 x 35.5ft
Speed 13-15 knots

Notes:
Chartered out at first, then a support ship during fisheries dispute. Sold 1972 for scrap.

Ship	Completion Date	Builder	Propulsion
WAVE CHIEF (A265)	1946	Harland & Wolff	Steam

Displacement 8097 tons gross   **Dimensions** 494 x 64 x 35.5ft
Speed 13-15 knots

Notes:
Also began career under charter. Later she ran ashore in Johore Straits and suffered bottom damage. Fisheries dispute 1958-61. In 1968 she escorted Sir Alec Rose in "Lively Lady" round Cape Horn. Sold 1975.

Ship	Completion Date	Builder	Propulsion
WAVE RULER (A212)	1946	Furness Shipbuilding	Steam

Displacement 8138 tons gross   **Dimensions** 494 x 64 x 35.5ft
Speed 13-15 knots

Notes:
Entered RFA Service after period on charter, went aground Swansea 1953 but was salved. Involved with fisheries dispute and the Christmas Islands H-Bomb test. Final assignment was as a fuelling hulk at Gan in 1971.

Ship	Completion Date	Builder	Propulsion
WAVE COMMANDER	1944	Furness Shipbuilding	Steam

Displacement 8141 tons gross   **Dimensions** 494 x 64 x 35.5ft
Speed 13-15 knots

Notes:
Was initially chartered out. In 1954 she was in collision in the Straits of Gibraltar. Scrapped 1959.

RFA Wave Ruler

Ship	Completion Date	Builder	Propulsion
WAVE CONQUERER	1944	Furness Shipbuilding	Steam

Displacement 8128 tons gross **Dimensions** 494 x 64 x 35.5ft
Speed 13-15 knots

Notes:
Entered RFA Service in 1946. Scrapped 1959.

Ship	Completion Date	Builder	Propulsion
WAVE DUKE (A246)	1944	Laing	Steam

Displacement 8199 tons gross **Dimensions** 494 x 64 x 35.5ft
Speed 13-15 knots

Notes:
RFA from 1946. Scrapped 1965.

RFA Wave Duke

Unmodified Ships were:-

Ship	Completion Date	Builder	Propulsion
WAVE EMPEROR	1944	Furness Shipbuilding	Steam

Displacement 8196 tons gross   **Dimensions** 494 x 64 x 35.5ft
Speed 13-15 knots

Notes:
Was ready in time to join the fleet in the war against Japan. Scrapped 1966.

RFA Wave Emperor (Nov 1946)

WAVE KING	1944	Harland & Wolff	Steam

Displacement 8159 tons gross   **Dimensions** 494 x 64 x 35.5ft
Speed 13-15 knots

Notes:
Was ready in time to join the fleet in the war against Japan. Scrapped 1966.

WAVE LIBERATOR	1944	Furness Shipbuilding	Steam

Displacement 8135 tons gross   **Dimensions** 494 x 64 x 35.5ft
Speed 13-15 knots

Notes:
Was built with a different design bridge: acquired for RFA Service 1946.
Sold 1956.

Ship	Completion Date	Builder	Propulsion
WAVE MONARCH	1944	Harland & Wolff	Steam

Displacement 8159 tons gross **Dimensions** 494 x 64 x 35.5ft
Speed 13-15 knots

Notes:
Was ready in time to join the fleet in the war against Japan. Sold 1960.

WAVE PROTECTOR	1944	Furness Shipbuilding	Steam

Displacement 8148 tons gross **Dimensions** 494 x 64 x 35.5ft
Speed 13-15 knots

Notes:
RFA Service from 1946. Her latter years spent as storage hulk at Malta. Scrapped 1963.

RFA Wave Protector (Feb 1953)

Ship	Completion Date	Builder	Propulsion
WAVE GOVERNOR	1945	Furness Shipbuilding	Steam

Displacement 8190 tons gross   **Dimensions** 494 x 64 x 35.5ft
Speed 13-15 knots

Notes:
Was ready in time to join the fleet in the war against Japan. Scrapped 1960-61.

RFA Wave Regent (Oct 1953)

WAVE REGENT	1945	Furness Shipbuilding	Steam

Displacement 8184 tons gross   **Dimensions** 494 x 64 x 35.5ft
Speed 13-15 knots

Notes:
Scrapped 1960-61.

RFA Wave Laird (Aug 1952)

Ship	Completion Date	Builder	Propulsion
WAVE LAIRD *(A119)*	1946	Laing	Steam

Displacement 8187 tons gross **Dimensions** 494 x 64 x 35.5ft
Speed 13-15 knots

Notes:
Was support ship to HMS "Protector" in Antarctica and ran supplies to the Falklands. Then took part in the 1958-61 fisheries dispute. Scrapped 1970.

Ship	Completion Date	Builder	Propulsion
WAVE PREMIER	1946	Furness Shipbuilding	Steam

Displacement 8175 tons gross **Dimensions** 494 x 64 x 35.5ft
Speed 13-15 knots

Notes:
Broken up in 1956.

Fleet Replenishment Ship

RFA Olna

Ship	Completion Date	Builder	Propulsion
OLNA II (A216)	1945	Swan Hunter	Turbo-Electric

Displacement 12667 tons gross   **Dimensions** 583 x 70 x 40.5 ft
Speed 16 knots

Notes:
She was commissioned into RN for the Pacific Fleet but transferred into RFA service in 1946. Her Hull (round petrol tanks) was armoured. Used for fuelling at sea experiments and lessons learnt were embodied in later classes. Scrapped 1966.

RFA Northmark as HMS Bulawayo (Oct 48)

Ship	Completion Date	Builder	Propulsion
NORTHMARK	1939	Schichau, Elbing	Steam

Displacement 10847 tons gross   **Dimensions** 584 x 72.5 x 30ft
Speed 21 knots

Notes:
Formerly German Fast Fleet Attendant oiler and supply ship—ex "Nordmark", ex "Westerwald". Seized as Naval prize in 1945 and was handed over to the RFA and renamed "Northmark" but was again renamed "HMS Bulawayo" in 1947. Fleet train 47-48. Reserve 1950. Arrived Dalmuir 4 Oct 1955 to be scrapped.

Ship	Completion Date	Builder	Propulsion
RIPPLEDYKE **(Ex Empire Tesbury)**	1946	Bartram	Steam

Displacement 975 tons gross   **Dimensions** 193 x 34 x 14.5 ft
Speed 10 knots

Notes:
RFA manned only in 1958 when sent to Gibraltar as oil hulk. Admiralty owned from 1949 but chartered out. Sold 1960 for service as a dredger at Palermo, Sicily.

The 1500 Ton Class

Ship	Completion Date	Builder	Propulsion
BIRCHOL (2) (A127)	1946	Lobnitz	Steam

Displacement 1440 tons gross **Dimensions** 231.5 x 38 x 17ft
Speed 12 knots

Notes:
Stationed at Hong Kong for many years. Sold Belgium 1969.

Ship	Completion Date	Builder	Propulsion
OAKOL (2) (A300)	1946	Lobnitz	Steam

Displacement 1440 tons gross **Dimensions** 231.5 x 38 x 17ft
Speed 12 knots

Notes:
Early years at Singapore. Sold Belgium 1969.

Ship	Completion Date	Builder	Propulsion
ROWANOL (A284)	1946	Lobnitz	Steam

Displacement 1440 tons gross **Dimensions** 231.5 x 38 x 17ft
Speed 12 knots

Notes:
Was built as "Ebonol" but name was changed when her predecessor was recovered from the Japanese. However, her new name "Cedarol" caused confusion with "Cedardale" and she was finally rechristened. Sold in 1971.

Ship	Completion Date	Builder	Propulsion
TEAKOL (3) (A167)	1946	Lobnitz	Steam

Displacement 1440 tons gross **Dimensions** 231.5 x 38 x 17ft
Speed 12 knots

Notes:
Her career was spent in home waters. Sold 1969.

RFA Birchol

The "Eddy" Class

Eight ships built as coastal tankers. Their lives were short due to the adoption of replenishment at sea as standard practice.

Ship	Completion Date	Builder	Propulsion
EDDYBEACH (A132)	1951	Caledon	Steam

Displacement 2157 tons gross **Dimensions** 288 x 46 x 18.5ft
Speed 12 knots

Notes:
Mediterranean service, mostly at Gibraltar where she also acted as water carrier. Sold to Greece 1964.

RFA Eddybay (Feb 1954)

EDDYBAY (A107)	1952	Caledon	Steam

Displacement 2156 tons gross **Dimensions** 288 x 46 x 18.5ft
Speed 12 knots

Notes:
Was stationed for three years, as petrol carrier for the RAF, at Gibraltar. Scrapped 1965.

RFA Eddycliff (Jan 1953)

Ship	Completion Date	Builder	Propulsion
EDDYCLIFF (A190)	1953	Blythswood	Steam

Displacement 2173 tons gross   **Dimensions** 288 x 46 x 18.5ft
Speed 12 knots

Notes:
Spent most of her time at Malta, where she was sold 1966.

Ship	Completion Date	Builder	Propulsion
EDDYCREEK (A258)	1953	Lobnitz	Steam

Displacement 2224 tons gross   **Dimensions** 288 x 46 x 18.5ft
Speed 12 knots

Notes:
Based at Hong Kong and sold there 1965.

RFA Eddycreek

Ship	Completion Date	Builder	Propulsion
EDDYROCK (A198)	1953	Blyth Drydock & Shipbuilding	Steam

Displacement 2173 tons gross   **Dimensions** 288 x 46 x 18.5ft
Speed 12 knots

Notes:
Stationed Singapore and involved in Indonesian confrontation. Scrapped 1967.

Ship	Completion Date	Builder	Propulsion
EDDYREEF (A202)	1953	Caledon	Steam

Displacement 2172 tons gross   **Dimensions** 288 x 46 x 18.5ft
Speed 12 knots

Notes:
Scrapped 1964.

RFA Eddyreef (Nov 1953)

RFA Eddyfirth — still in service in the 80's.

Ship	Completion Date	Builder	Propulsion
EDDYFIRTH (A261)	1954	Lobnitz	Steam

Displacement 2222 tons gross   **Dimensions** 288 x 46 x 18.5ft
Speed 12 knots

Notes:
Supported Minesweepers in the Mediterranean & UK coastal freighting.
Scrapped 1982.

Ship	Completion Date	Builder	Propulsion
EDDYNESS (A295)	1954	Blyth	Steam

Displacement 2172 tons gross   **Dimensions** 288 x 46 x 18.5ft
Speed 12 knots

Notes:
Served principally in home waters until scrapped 1970.

Tankers Acquired during Korean War

Ship	Completion Date	Builder	Propulsion
SURF PATROL (A357)	1951	Bartram	Diesel

Displacement 7742 tons gross   **Dimensions** 470 x 60 x 27.5ft
Speed 15.4 knots

Notes:
Built for Polish Owners. Ex "Tatry". Sold to Panama 1969.

Ship	Completion Date	Builder	Propulsion
SURF PIONEER (A367)	1951	Bartram	Diesel

Displacement 7742 tons gross   **Dimensions** 470 x 60 x 27.5ft
Speed 12.5 knots

Notes:
Ex "Beskidy". Sold to Spain 1969.

RFA Surf Patrol

The Third "Leaf" Class

These seven broadly similar ships were chartered as replacement for the "Dales" and "Waves". Although intended primarily for freighting, most were capable of RAS.

Ship	Completion Date	Builder	Propulsion
BRAMBLELEAF (2) (A81)	1954	Furness Shipbuilding & Engineering	Diesel

Displacement 12500 tons gross **Dimensions** 557.5 x 68 x 38ft
Speed 14.5 knots

Notes:
On bareboat charter 1959-70.

Ship	Completion Date	Builder	Propulsion
APPLELEAF (2) (A83)	1955	Bartram	Diesel

Displacement 11588 tons gross **Dimensions** 557.5 x 68 x 38ft
Speed 14.5 knots

Notes:
On bareboat charter 1959-72

Ship	Completion Date	Builder	Propulsion
BAYLEAF (2) (A79)	1955	Furness Shipbuilding & Engineering	Diesel

Displacement 12500 tons gross **Dimensions** 556.5 x 71.5 x 39ft
Speed 14.5 knots

Notes:
On bareboat charter 1959-73.

RFA Brambleleaf arrives in the Suez Canal.

RFA Orangeleaf (Nov 1968)

Ship	Completion Date	Builder	Propulsion
ORANGELEAF (2) (A80)	1955	Furness Shipbuilding & Engineering	Diesel

Displacement 12481 tons gross   **Dimensions** 556.5 x 71.5 x 39ft
Speed 14.5 knots

Notes:
She suffered a tank explosion at Falmouth 1969, was chartered four years after building and fitted for abeam fuelling. Returned to owners May 1978.

Ship	Completion Date	Builder	Propulsion
CHERRYLEAF (2) (A82)	1953	Laing	Diesel

Displacement 12402 tons gross   **Dimensions** 568 x 72 x 39ft
Speed 15 knots

Notes:
Ex "Laurelwood". On bareboat charter 1959-66. Sold to Greek Interests.

RFA Pearleaf — before being converted to full RAS specifications.

Ship	Completion Date	Builder	Propulsion
PEARLEAF (2) (A77)	1960	Blythswood Shipbuilding	Diesel

Displacement 12353 tons gross **Dimensions** 568 x 72 x 39ft
Speed 15 knots

Ship	Completion Date	Builder	Propulsion
PLUMLEAF (2) (A78)	1961	Blyth Drydock	Diesel

Displacement 12692 tons gross **Dimensions** 568 x 72 x 39ft
Speed 15 knots

Notes:
Both these ships were taken over while building on 20 years bareboat charter and fitted for abeam fuelling. Classified as "Freighting Tankers", their disposal was averted by the Falklands Crisis. The latter was the first ship to pass through the Suez Canal when it re-opened 1975. Both still in service (1985).

Ship	Completion Date	Builder	Propulsion
CHERRYLEAF (3) (A82)	1963	Emdem	Diesel

Displacement 13721 tons gross **Dimensions** 559 x 72 x 30
Speed 14.5 knots

Notes:
Ex MV "Overseas Adventurer" chartered 1973-79. Was towed across the Indian Ocean by "Hebe" in 1976.

RFA Cherryleaf

Fleet Tankers
The "Tide" Class

Between 1955 and 1956 the first four tankers to be designed specifically for fleet oiling duties entered service. They were built to identical specifications and all fitted with automatic jackstay tensioning winches to facilitate abeam fuelling in severe weather.

In 1963 two improved "Tide" class tankers joined the RFA Fleet: These were given three RAS derrick rigs on each side which, combined with astern arrangements, allowed three ships to be fuelled simultaneously. Three grades of fuel, together with water could be supplied, as well as lub oils, general and victualling stores. A hangar and flight deck could accommodate three helicopters.

Ship	Completion Date	Builder	Propulsion
TIDEREACH (A96)	1955 Richardson	Swan Hunter & Wigham	Steam

Displacement 13516 tons gross **Dimensions** 583 x 71 x 40.5ft
Speed 18 knots

Notes:
Scrapped 1979.

TIDEAUSTRAL (A95)	1955	Harland & Wolff	Steam

Displacement 13165 tons gross **Dimensions** 583 x 71 x 40.5ft
Speed 18 knots

Notes:
Built for RAN but lent to RN till 1962. Was renamed HMAS "Supply" when delivered to RAN.

RFA Tidereach sails up the Johore Straits to Singapore Naval Base (1973).

RFA Tideflow (& HMS Triumph)

Ship	Completion Date	Builder	Propulsion
TIDEFLOW (A97)	1956	Thompson	Steam

Displacement 13718 tons gross **Dimensions** 583 x 71 x 40.5ft
Speed 18 knots

Notes:
Was named "Tiderace" 'till 1958. Scrapped 1976.

TIDESURGE (A98)	1956	Laing	Steam

Displacement 13732 tons gross **Dimensions** 583 x 71 x 40.5ft
Speed 18 knots

Notes:
Was named "Tiderange" till 1958. She assisted Lord Shackleton's survey of the Falklands. Scrapped in 1977.

SECOND GROUP

TIDEPOOL (A76)	1963	Hawthorn Leslie	Steam

Displacement 14130 tons gross **Dimensions** 583 x 71 x 40.5ft
Speed 18 knots

Notes:
Supported the Beira patrol in 1966, ran aground 1975 in Firth of Clyde. Took part in the 1976 'Cod War'. Was sold to Chile in 1982.

TIDESPRING (A75)	1963	Hawthorn Leslie	Steam

Displacement 14130 tons gross **Dimensions** 583 x 71 x 40.5ft
Speed 18 knots

Notes:
She is the only ship of the class remaining in service (1985) having been reprieved by the Falklands Crisis. She helped with the relief of Rodriguez Is after a hurricane in 1973.

RFA Tidepool

RFA Tidespring, her hull weatherworn and rusting, arriving at Singapore after a record ninety days on the Beira patrol. She berthed with only one sack of potatoes left to feed the 110 officers and men on board and sent a radio message for barbers to meet the ship to cut the hair of the crew which had grown to shoulder length.

The "Olwen" Class

A bigger and faster version of the "Tides". This class is fitted to carry stores as well as fuel, and strengthened against ice. Helicopters can be operated and embarked. Classified as 'Large Fleet Tankers'.

Ship	Completion Date	Builder	Propulsion
OLWEN (2) (A122)	1965	Hawthorne Leslie	Steam

Displacement 18604 tons gross **Dimensions** 648 x 84 x 44ft
Speed 19 knots

Notes:
Was named "Olynthus" (2) till 1967. Name caused confusion with HMS "Olympus". Provided RAS for frigates in the 1976 'Cod War'. Two years later, she grounded without damage on the Shambles. Still in service (1985).

Ship	Completion Date	Builder	Propulsion
OLMEDA (A124)	1965	Swan Hunter & Wigham Richardson	Steam

Displacement 18586 tons gross **Dimensions** 648 x 84 x 44ft
Speed 19 knots

Notes:
Was named "Oleander" (2) till 1967. Named caused confusion with HMS "Leander". Still in service (1985).

Ship	Completion Date	Builder	Propulsion
OLNA (3) (A123)	1966	Hawthorn Leslie	Steam

Displacement 18582 tons gross **Dimensions** 648 x 84 x 44ft
Speed 19 knots

Notes:
Rescued the entire crew of a ship that sank in the Arabian Sea during severe weather and poor visability in 1966. Still in service (1985).

RFA Oleander — later named Olmeda

RFA Olwen

Post War "Dale" Class

When the number of overseas bases was being reduced, the Admiralty realised that extra tanker capacity would be needed and decided to charter three super tankers to ensure the continued supply of fuel East of Suez. They were classified as "Mobile Bulk Tankers".

Ship	Completion Date	Builder	Propulsion
DERWENTDALE (2) (A221)	1965	Hatachi Zosen, Innoshima	Diesel

Displacement 42504 tons gross 67,729 tons deadweight
Dimensions 799 x 117.8 x 55.5ft   **Speed** 15.5 knots

Notes:
Ex Halcyon Breeze. RFA service 1967-74

Ship	Completion Date	Builder	Propulsion
DEWDALE (2) (A219)	1965	Harland & Wolff	Diesel

Displacement 35805 tons gross 60,600 tons deadweight
Dimensions 774.5 x 107.8 x 55ft   **Speed** 15 knots

Notes:
RFA service from 1967 on bareboat charter. Aden operations 1968.

Ship	Completion Date	Builder	Propulsion
ENNERDALE (2)	1963	Keiler Howaldtswerke	Diesel

Displacement 30112 tons gross 47,470 tons deadweight
Dimensions 710 x 98.5 x 52ft   **Speed** 15.5 knots

Notes:
Bareboat chartered for RFA service 1967. Ship's company awarded Wilkinson Sword of peace for rescuing staff of weather station at Gough Island in severe weather. A little later in June 1970, she was lost after striking an unchartered rock off the Seychelles but all hands reached Mahé safely. Her hull was destroyed by bombing after the oil slick had been cleared by the RN. This vessel's RFA career lasted less than three years.

RFA Derwentdale — somewhat larger than the previous ship of the name.

RFA Dewdale (Feb 1968)

RFA Ennerdale (Sept 1969)

99

The "Rover" Class

Classified as "Small Fleet Tankers", this class was specifically designed to operate in close support of fleet units. Fitted for RAS abeam and over bow and stern, as well as Vertrep, these vessels carry diesel, aviation fuel, petrol, lub oils, fresh water and limited dry cargo and refrigerated stores.

Ship	Completion Date	Builder	Propulsion
GREEN ROVER (A268)	1969	Swan Hunter	Diesel

Displacement 7570 tons gross   **Dimensions** 465.3 x 62.7ft **Speed** 18 knots

Notes:
In 1972 her flight deck was used successfully for harrier landing and take-off trials.

Ship	Completion Date	Builder	Propulsion
GREY ROVER (A 269)	1970	Swan Hunter	Diesel

Displacement 7570 tons gross   **Dimensions** 465.3 x 62.7ft **Speed** 18 knots

Notes:
Was present during the run down of the Malta Naval Base in 1977.

RFA Green Rover

Ship	Completion Date	Builder	Propulsion
BLUE ROVER (A270)	1970	Swan Hunter	Diesel

Displacement 7570 tons gross   **Dimensions** 465.3 x 62.7ft **Speed** 18 knots

Notes:
Supported the Royal Yacht "Britannia" during cruises to the Pacific and Singapore in 1971 and 1972: during the former she broke down and was towed 1120 miles by "Britannia".

Ship	Completion Date	Builder	Propulsion
GOLD ROVER (A271)	1974	Swan Hunter	Diesel

Displacement 7570 tons gross   **Dimensions** 465.3 x 62.7ft **Speed** 18 knots

Notes:
In 1975 temporarily flew the flag of FO 2nd flotilla in the Pacific. During that deployment she steamed 406,000 miles and visited 60 ports. Successfully demonstrated the possibility of replenishing a commercial tanker underway.

Ship	Completion Date	Builder	Propulsion
BLACK ROVER (A273)	1974	Swan Hunter	Diesel

Displacement 7570 tons gross   **Dimensions** 465.3 x 62.7ft **Speed** 18 knots

Notes:
Was in Malta for the independence ceremonies and assisted with the evacuation when Turkey invaded Cyprus in 1974. Three years later she accompanied HMS "Kent" on a proving cruise through the Bosphorous to the Black Sea.

RFA Blue Rover (1979)

RFA Gold Rover (1974)

New "Leaf" Class

This group of ships was acquired primarily for consolidating fleet tankers and replenishing warships at sea. They carry diesel and aviation fuel.

Ship	Completion Date	Builder	Propulsion
APPLELEAF (3) (A79)	1980	Cammell Laird	Diesel

Displacement 19975 tons gross **Dimensions** 564.3 x 85.7ft **Speed** 15 knots

Notes:
Ex "Hudson Cavalier", taken over by the M.O.D. when part completed.

BRAMBLELEAF (3) (A81)	1980	Cammell Laird	Diesel

Displacement 19975 tons gross **Dimensions** 564.3 x 85.7ft **Speed** 15 knots

Notes:
Ex "Hudson Deep", taken over by the MO.D. when part completed.

BAYLEAF (3) (A109)	1982	Cammell Laird	Diesel

Displacement 19975 tons gross **Dimensions** 564.3 x 85.7ft **Speed** 15 knots

Notes
On charter.

ORANGELEAF (3) (A119)	1982	Cammell Laird	Diesel

Displacement 19975 tons gross **Dimensions** 564.3 x 85.7ft **Speed** 15 knots

Notes:
Was formerly M/V "Balder London". Refitted 1985 to full RAS specifications.

RFA Appleleaf (1983)

Miscellaneous Tankers

Ship	Completion Date	Builder	Propulsion
DANMARK	1931	Burmeister & Wain	Diesel
Displacement 5419 tons gross	**Dimensions** 490 x 35ft		**Speed** 11 knots

Notes:
Torpedoed 1940; forward part salvaged and repaired, then stationed Scapa Flow as fuel hulk. Sold 1948 to Shell-Mex for use as oil storage depot at Dublin.

Ship	Completion Date	Builder	Propulsion
BERTA	1927	Harland & Wolff	Steam
Displacement 2600 tons gross	**Dimensions** 305 x 50 x 15ft		
Speed knots			

Notes:
On charter and RFA manned during WW II. Employed mainly in Plymouth area.

Ship	Completion Date	Builder	Propulsion
INGEBORG	1937	J L Meyer	Diesel
Displacement 479 tons gross	**Dimensions** 159 x 25 x 11ft		
Speed 10 knots			

Notes:
Taken over from Dutch Owners during WW II and handed back afterwards.

Ship	Completion Date	Builder	Propulsion
EMPIRE SALVAGE	1940	Rotterdam Dry Dock Co Ltd	Diesel
Displacement 10476 tons gross	**Dimensions** 496 x 73 x 35ft		
Speed 12.5 knots			

Notes:
Commandeered by Germans from Dutch and renamed "Lotharingen". Used as supply ship for "Bismarck"; captured by "Ark Royal" and converted to RFA tanker. Used for experiments with, and development of the German rubber hose method of RAS. Served in Canada, Burma landings and Far East until returned to owners in 1946.

PART II
Stores Support Ships

Ship	Completion Date	Builder	Propulsion
RELIANCE	1910	Connell	Steam

Displacement 9220 tons gross   **Dimensions** 469.5 x 58ft
Speed 11 knots

Notes:
RN Repair ship 1913-16 then to RFA service. Sold to Italian Owners 1921.

BACCHUS	1915	WM Hamilton	Steam

Displacement 2000 tons gross   **Dimensions** 295 x 49 x 12.5ft
Speed 10 knots

Notes:
Originally a repair ship. Distillation ship/water carrier till 1917 then stores carrier. Egypt 1916-18; North Russia 1919; East Indies 1922-23. Then Chatham — Malta stores run until Abyssinian War when again distilling ship in Egypt. Sunk as a target November 1938 by HMS "Dunedin" 10 miles off Alderney after being damaged as bombing target.

DEMETER	1920	Gotaverken	Diesel

Displacement 5646 tons gross   **Dimensions** 426 x 56 x 26ft
Speed 11 knots

Notes:
Taken up as a store and victualling hulk at Scapa Flow after being mined in entrance to Mersey 1940 (as M/V Buenos Aires).

RFA Bacchus (1)

RFA Reliant (at Malta)

Ship	Completion Date	Builder	Propulsion
RELIANT	1922	Furness Shipbuilding	Steam

Displacement 7928 tons gross   **Dimensions** 450 x 58 x 38ft
Speed 14 knots

Notes:
Purchased and converted 1933. Served Mediterranean fleet and East Indies. Sold to Maltese owners 1948.

Ship	Completion Date	Builder	Propulsion
BACCHUS (2)	1936	Caledon Shipbuilding & Engineering	Steam

Displacement 3154 tons gross   **Dimensions** 337 x 49 x 23ft
Speed 12 knots

Notes:
In 1939 she fought and drove off a U-boat. Stationed at Clyde and Scapa Flow until 1941. East Indies 1942-45 then with Pacific Fleet train, also acting as distilling ship. From 1946 on run between UK, Mediterranean and Far East. Sold to Singapore Owners 1962.

RFA Bacchus (2) at Malta

Ship	Completion Date	Builder	Propulsion
INDUSTRY	1901	Beardmore	Steam

Displacement 800 GRT   **Dimensions** 196 x 30 x 18.5ft   **Speed** 10 knots

Notes:
Ex Q Ship "Tay" and "Tyne". RFA manned from 1914 and torpedoed 1918 but reached harbour. Sold 1919.

Ship	Completion Date	Builder	Propulsion
ROBERT MIDDLETON (A241)	1938	Grangemouth Dockyard	Diesel

Displacement 1124 tons gross   **Dimensions** 222.5 x 35 x 18ft
Speed 12 knots

Ship	Completion Date	Builder	Propulsion
ROBERT DUNDAS (A204)	1938	Grangemouth Dockyard	Diesel

Displacement 1125 tons gross   **Dimensions** 222.5 x 35 x 18ft
Speed 12 knots

Notes:
Sister ships, classed as "Coastal Stores Carriers". "R Dundas" entered RFA service 1940 and served in Mediterranean and at Normandy Landings. Sold 1972. "R Middleton" also was at Normandy invasion. Sold to Greek Owners 1976.

RFA Robert Middleton (Nov 1952)

The "Fort" Class
(See also under Armament Storeships)

Canadian built Victory type. They were originally intended for operations in Europe and Pacific but their low speed was a handicap and they were used instead as stores issuing ships with the Pacific Fleet train, manned commercially as Merchant Fleet Auxiliaries (MFAs).

Ship	Completion Date	Builder	Propulsion
FORT BEAUHARNOIS	1944	West Coast Shipbuilders	Steam

Displacement 7253 tons gross **Dimensions** 440.3 x 57 x 35ft
Speed 10 - 11 knots

Notes:
Entered RFA Service 1950 and employed Chatham — Gibraltar — Malta. At Christmas Island nuclear test. Freighting UK — Far East 1960-62 and sold 1962 for scrap.

Ship	Completion Date	Builder	Propulsion
FORT CHARLOTTE (A236)	1944	Vancouver Drydock Co	Steam

Displacement 7214 tons gross **Dimensions** 440.3 x 57 x 35ft
Speed 10 - 11 knots

Notes:
Was an RFA from 1948. Took part in Korean War. Also at Christmas Island nuclear test, and on UK — Malta run until 1960 when she was transferred to Hong Kong. Sold 1967.

Ship	Completion Date	Builder	Propulsion
FORT CONSTANTINE	1944	Vancouver Drydock Co	Steam

Displacement 7221 tons gross **Dimensions** 440.3 x 57 x 35ft
Speed 10 - 11 knots

Notes:
Freighting to Mediterranean and Far East 1950-56; Christmas Island test 1956 then on Chatham — Malta run. Sold to German Owners 1969.

RFA Fort Beauharnois (Oct 1952)

RFA Fort Duquesne carries out early helicopter replenishment trials.

Ship	Completion Date	Builder	Propulsion
FORT DUNVEGAN (A160)	1944	Burrard	Steam

Displacement 7225 tons gross **Dimensions** 440.3 x 57 x 35ft
Speed 10 - 11 knots

Notes:
Entered RFA service 1951 and was the first ship to fly the Commodore's Burgee. On UK — Malta run until 1960 when transferred to Far East. Scrapped 1968.

FORT DUQUESNE (A229)	1944	West Coast Shipbuilders	Steam

Displacement 7220 tons gross **Dimensions** 440.3 x 57 x 35ft
Speed 10 - 11 knots

Notes:
RFA from 1947 and attached to Mediterranean Fleet. In 1951 used for important trials of vertical replenishment (Vertrep), using helicopters for which a flight deck was fitted; they were successful and the system was adopted widely later. Involved in Suez operations 1956. Scrapped 1967.

Naval Aviation Store Carriers

Ship	Completion Date	Builder	Propulsion
SEAFOX	1946	J Pollack	Diesel

Displacement 711 tons gross   **Dimensions** 210 x 35ft   **Speed** 10.5 knots

Notes:
Sister ships "Roc", "Skua" and "Blackburn" were RN vessels. Fitted for ferrying aircraft and general stores. Employed mostly between Northern Ireland and West Coast of England and Scotland until sold in 1958.

Ship	Completion Date	Builder	Propulsion
RELIANT (2) (A84)	1954	J Laing	Diesel

Displacement 7928 tons gross   **Dimensions** 469 x 61.5 x 40ft
Speed 17 knots

Notes:
Purchased and converted 1957. Also carried some victualing stores. Served mainly in Far East. Scrapped 1976. Known as "The Yacht" throughout the service.

RFA Reliant (Aug 1969)

STORES VESSELS

Ship	Completion Date	Builder	Propulsion
BACCHUS (3) (A404)	1962	Henry Robb	Diesel

Displacement 4823 tons gross **Dimensions** 379 x 55 x 31ft
Speed 15 knots

Ship	Completion Date	Builder	Propulsion
HEBE (A406)	1962	Henry Robb	Diesel

Displacement 4823 tons gross **Dimensions** 379 x 55 x 31ft
Speed 15 knots

Notes:
Both were on bareboat charter from B.I.S.N. Co and designed to carry dry
and refrigerated cargo plus lub oil and water. Specially designed containers
were carried. "Bacchus" was used to transport stores between naval bases
at home and overseas. Returned to owners 1981. "Hebe" towed
"Cherryleaf" across Indian Ocean in 1976 and two years later was severely
damaged by fire at Gibraltar. Charter terminated same year.

RFA Bacchus

Armament Stores Issuing Ships (ASIS)

RFA Amherst (June 1953)

Ship	Completion Date	Builder	Propulsion
AMHERST	1936	Blythswood	Steam

Displacement 3496 tons gross **Dimensions** 315 x 45 x 24.5ft
Speed 13.5 knots

Notes:
Taken into RFA service 1951 as a replacement for the "Bedenham" (PAS) which had been destroyed by explosion in Gibraltar. On UK — Gibraltar — Malta run until scrapped in 1963-64.

The "Fort" Class
(For particulars, see under Storeships)

Ship	Completion Date	Builder	Propulsion
FORT LANGLEY (A230)	1945	Victoria Machinery Depot	Steam

Displacement 7285 tons gross   **Dimensions** 441 x 57 x 35ft
Speed 10 - 11 knots

Notes:
Transferred to RFA as an armament stores issuing ship 1954. Scrapped 1970 in Bilbao Spain.

RFA Fort Langley

RFA Fort Rosalie

Ship	Completion Date	Builder	Propulsion
FORT ROSALIE (A186)	1945	United Shipyards, Montreal	Steam

Displacement 7374 tons gross **Dimensions** 441 x 57 x 35ft
Speed 10 - 11 knots

Notes:
After war service as Naval Stores Issuing ship (MFA) with fleet train converted to ASIS (RFA). Far East 1949-51: Christmas Island nuclear tests; used to return ammunition from Australia and South Africa. Scrapped 1973.

Ship	Completion Date	Builder	Propulsion
FORT SANDUSKY (A316)	1944	United Shipyards, Montreal	Steam

Displacement 7374 tons gross **Dimensions** 441 x 57 x 35ft
Speed 10 - 11 knots

Notes:
In Far East as ASIS (MFA). After transfer to RFA served mostly on Far East station except for Suez operation 1956. Also returned ammunition from Australia.

RFA Retainer

Ship	Completion Date	Builder	Propulsion
RESURGENT (A280)	1951	Scotts Shipbuilding	Diesel

Displacement 9357 tons gross
Speed 15 knots.

Ship	Completion Date	Builder	Propulsion
RETAINER (A329)	1950	Scotts Shipbuilding	Diesel

Dimensions 477 x 62 x 35ft

Displacement 9357 tons gross
Speed 15 knots.

Dimensions 477 x 62 x 35ft

Notes:
Both were purchased from China Navigation Co 1952 and RFA manned from 1957. They carried some victualling stores as well as ammunition and operated principally in the Far East. Replaced by new Fort Class.

Fleet Replenishment Ships

Ship	Completion Date	Builder	Propulsion
LYNESS (A339)	1966	Swan Hunter	Diesel
STROMNESS (A344)	1967	Swan Hunter	Diesel
TARBATNESS (A345)	1967	Swan Hunter	Diesel

Displacement 12,359 tons gross   **Dimensions** 523.5 x 72.5 x 44.5ft
Speed 17 knots

Notes:
Replacement for the "Forts" these "floating supermarkets" could carry thousands of items of Naval stores and provisions to enable the fleet to remain at sea for lengthy periods. "Tarbatness" also carried air stores. Capable of Vertrep but no hangar. "Lyness" sold to US Sealift Command 1981. "Stromness" and "Tarbatness" followed later.

RFA Tarbatness (Aug 1967)

RFA Resource (May 1975)

RESOURCE (A480)	1967	Scotts	Steam
REGENT (A486)	1967	Harland & Wolff	Steam

Displacement 18029 tons gross   **Dimensions** 640 x 77 x 49.5ft
Speed 21 knots

Notes:
The only RFA ships with an RN helicopter embarked permanently. A full range of armament stores and ammunition is carried, together with limited stores and provisions.

Ship	Completion Date	Builder	Propulsion
FORT GRANGE (A385)	1978	Scott Lithgow	Diesel
FORT AUSTIN (A386)	1979	Scott Lithgow	Diesel

Displacement 16009 tons gross **Dimensions** 603.9 x 79.2ft
Speed 20 knots

Notes:
Both carry a wide range of armament stores, ammunition, naval stores, dry and refrigerated provisions and NAAFI stores for RAS. Full hangar and maintenance facilities are provided for up to four Sea King helicopters to be used for A/S protection as well as Vertrep. At the onset of the Falklands operation, "Fort Austin" was the first surface ship to sail south and she, and "Fort Grange", provided concentrated flight deck facilities for ASW helicopters over long periods during the conflict.

RFA Fort Grange

PART III Miscellaneous Ships
Landing Ships, Logistic (LSL)

Ship	Completion Date	Builder	Propulsion
EMPIRE GULL (L3523)	1945	Davie Shipbuilding Quebec	Steam

Displacement 4258 tons gross   **Dimensions** 346.5 x 56.1ft   **Speed** 10 knots

Notes:
Ex LST 3523. First commissioned as HMS "Trouncer". Transferred to MOD (Army) 1956 and renamed "Empire Gull", and to RFA service 1970. After service in Mediterranean, operated the Marchwood — Antwerp and Liverpool — Belfast runs. Scrapped 1978.

RFA Sir Bedivere

Ship	Completion Date	Builder	Propulsion
SIR LANCELOT (L3029)	1964	Fairfield	Diesel
SIR GALAHAD (L3005)	1966	Stephen	Diesel
SIR BEDIVERE (L3004)	1967	Stephen	Diesel
SIR TRISTRAM (L3505)	1967	Hawthorn	Diesel
SIR GERAINT (L3027)	1967	Stephen	Diesel
SIR PERCIVALE (L3036)	1968	Hawthorn	Diesel

Displacement 4500 tons **Dimensions** 415.8 x 59.4ft **Speed** 17 knots

Notes:
Designed as multi-purpose troop and heavy vehicle carriers, with bow and stern ramps. They joined the RFA service in 1970, having been operated previously by the B.I.S.N. Co for the Army (a greatly respected historical connection). They are still tasked by the Army. Helicopters can be operated from the tank deck. These ships gave valuable service in the Falklands in 1982 where "Sir Galahad" was lost with heavy casualties and "Sir Tristram" severely damaged; the latter was rebuilt in 1983-85.

RFA Sir Caradoc

Ship	Completion Date	Builder	Propulsion
SIR CARADOC (L3552)	1972	Trosvik Verksted, Norway	Diesel
Displacement 1899 tons gross		**Dimensions** 409.2ft long	**Speed** 16 knots
SIR LAMORAK (L3532)	1972	Ankerlokken Verft Floro, Sweden	Diesel
Displacement 1591 tons gross		**Dimensions** 355.4ft long	**Speed** 18 knots

Notes:
"Sir Caradoc" was built as 'Grey Master"; "Sir Lamorak" as "Lanu", her name on chartering was "Lakespan Ontario". Both are on bareboat charter as stop gap replacements for "Sir Tristram" and "Sir Galahad" but proved unsuitable for the South Atlantic. Employed on Marchwood — Antwerp freight run for the Army.

Helicopter/Aircraft Support Ships

Ship	Completion Date	Builder	Propulsion
ENGADINE (KO8)	1967	Robb	Diesel

Displacement 6384 tons gross   **Dimensions** 420 x 58ft   **Speed** 16 knots

Notes:
Specially built for RFA service (but with embarked RN personnel) to provide training ship for helicopter crews operating in deep waters well away from coasts. Can operate up to six helicopters and often embarks pilotless target aircraft for exercises, for which a hangar is provided above main hangar.

RFA Engadine (Oct 1975)

RFA Reliant (1984)

Ship	Completion Date	Builder	Propulsion
RELIANT (3) **(A131)**	1977	Gdansk, Poland Converted by Cammell Laird	Diesel

Displacement 27,867 tons gross   **Dimensions** 673.2 x 102.3ft
Speed 21 knots

Notes:
Came into RFA service 1983 but served in Falklands War as the chartered Merchant ship "Astronomer". Armament 4 x 20mm and five Sea King helicopters. Was designed to provide additional helicopter operating capability and stores support in South Atlantic waters. A similar second ship (Contender Bezant) has recently been purchased for conversion at a British yard, and will be named RFA "Argus". She will eventually replace "Engadine" in the RFA fleet.

Forward Support Ship

Ship	Completion Date	Builder	Propulsion
DILIGENCE (A132)	1981	Oresund-svarvet	Electric drive

Displacement 5814 GRT **Dimensions** 366 x 67ft **Speed** 15.5 knots

Notes:
Converted 1984. Had served in Falklands campaign as "Stena Inspector". Deployed to South Atlantic with RN maintenance unit embarked.

RFA Diligence (Jan 1985)

Hospital Ships

Maine has been the traditional name of RN hospital ships since the Boer War when an SS "Maine" was lent free of charge to the Army by the President of the American Atlantic Transport line. In 1901, she was presented to the Admiralty.

Ship	Completion Date	Builder	Propulsion
MAINE (1)	1887	Wm Gray & Co Ltd	Steam

Displacement 2816 tons gross   **Dimensions** 315 x 40 x 20ft
Speed 11 knots

Notes:
Absorbed into the new RFA service in 1905. She served in South Africa and was then sent to China for the Boxer Rebellion. Wrecked in fog off the Isle of Mull 1914 without loss of life.

MAINE (2)	1906	Henderson	Steam

Displacement 4688 tons gross   **Dimensions** 404.5 x 53 x 27ft
Speed 12.5 knots

Notes:
Acquired by Admiralty 1913 and converted at Pembroke Dock to hospital ship "Mediator". Rechristened on loss of former "Maine". However, she proved unsatisfactory and was then sold back to previous owners in 1916.

BERBICE	1909	Harland & Wolff Co Ltd	Steam

Displacement 2379 tons gross   **Dimensions** 300 x 38 x 23 ft
Speed 12 knots

Notes:
Ex-Army hospital ship. On hire to the Army from 1915-21. RFA 1919-21 only. Sold to UK Owners 1922. Was replaced by "Maine" (3).

Maine (3) (June 1933)

Ship	Completion Date	Builder	Propulsion
MAINE (3)	1902	Fairfield	Steam

Displacement 5891 tons gross   **Dimensions** 401 x 52 x 34ft
Speed 13 knots

Notes:
Built as "Panama" by Fairfield. Purchased by Admiralty in 1920 and in service 1922 after conversion. She was stationed mostly in the Mediterranean but was on the China station for some years. During Spanish Civil War she transported 6574 refugees of 41 nationalities. During WW II she tended more than 13,000 patients based at one time at Alexandria evacuating wounded from the eighth army. In 1941 "Maine" was severely damaged in an air raid but without harm to patients—although four crew were killed. In 1946 she was sent to help with the casualties from the Corfu Channel incident. Scrapped 1948.

MAINE (4)	1925	Ansaldo Soc Anon	Steam

Displacement 7515 tons gross   **Dimensions** 447 x 52.5 x 36ft
Speed 12 knots.

Notes:
Built as "Leonardo da Vinci". Captured at Massawa 1941 and converted (1943) to Army hospital ship "Empire Clyde". Transferred to Admiralty 1945 and to RFA service 1948 when re-named "Maine". She repatriated Australians from Pacific Theatre and was base hospital ship Hong Kong. During Korean War, she evacuated more than 13,000 casualties. Scrapped 1954.

RFA Maine at Malta (1949)

Miscellaneous

These ships and craft were RFA manned at times, which justifies their inclusion in this book.

Royal Research Ships.

Ship	Completion Date	Builder	Propulsion
DISCOVERY II	1929	Ferguson	Steam

Displacement 1036 tons gross   **Dimensions** 260.7 x 36.3ft   **Speed** 13 knots

Notes:
Given Suffix II because Captain Scott's "Discovery" was still in service for the Falklands Islands Government. Transferred to RFA service 1950. Scrapped 1962.

Ship	Completion Date	Builder	Propulsion
DISCOVERY	1962	Hall Russell	Diesel-Electric

Displacement 2667 tons gross   **Dimensions** 260.7 x 46.2ft
Speed 14 knots

Salvage Ships

RACER: used in 1917 to recover gold from the "Laurentic" sunk by a mine off Ireland. Ex Mariner Class sloop built at Devonport. 970 tons. Launched 1884. Converted to Salvage vessel 1917. Sold 1928.

King Salvor Class
1440 tons displacement   217 x 37 x 13ft   Steam Propulsion   12 knots
Completed 1942-5   Simons and Gocle

King Salvor	Salvestor	Salventure
Ocean Salvor	Salvictor	Salviking
Prince Salvor	Salvigil	
Salvage Duke	Salviola	
Salvalour	Sea Salvor	

Note: Salverdant completed as HMS Reclaim 1948. King Salvor was later HMS Kingfisher.

Salveda
1250 tons displacement   194 x 34 x 11ft   Steam propulsion   12 knots
Completed 1943   Cammell Laird.

Some Ships with limited RFA Service

WW I

Medway Ferries: **Waterwich, Wave (renamed Wayward 1919)**

Grand Fleet Torpedo Depot Ships: **Aro, Sobo, Sokoto**

Water Distilling Vessels: **Polmont, Polavon, Polgowan**

Store Carrier: **Polshannon**

Accommodation Ship: **Princetown**

Balloon Ship: **Canning**

Salvage Craft, Tugs and Others: **Lucia, Manica, Sun Hill, Caribbean, City of Oxford, Montcalm, Hungerford, Blackstone, Merryweather, Dapper, Holdfast, Fidget, Limpet, Messenger, Mollusc, Standfast, Volunteer, Thrush, Bullfrog, Steady, Anchorite, Melita, Hughly, Winkle, Victorious II, Slitigen, Reindeer, Innisfree.**

WW II

Water Carriers: **Freshbrook, Freshburn, Freshener, Freshnet, Freshford, Freshlake, Freshmere, Freshpond, Freshpool, Freshspray, Freshspring, Freshtarn, Freshwater, Freshwell, Spa, Spabeck, Spabrook, Spaburn, Spalake, Spapool.**

Tugs

A number of tugs have served under the RFA ensign. Readers should consult "50 Years of Naval Tugs" (published by Maritime Books) for details.

PHOTOLIBRARY
The RFA at Work . . . .

From early days of embarking coal (here HMS New Zealand carries out trials) the procedure for replenishing warships has advanced considerably . . . . .

. . . . . to early fuelling experiments. Here RFA Arndale floats a hose astern to a Hunt Class Destroyer.

Over the years Replenishment at Sea became a well proven method of keeping tanks and store rooms full.

Here (left to right) HMS Devonshire, RFA Olwen, HMS Hermes & RFA Lyness transfer fuel & stores during a NATO exercise.

Today . . . . . the helicopter plays a major part in many replenishment operations.

Other RFA's have been used to conduct trials with other aircraft—here a Harrier onboard RFA Green Rover. More and more RFA's now have the ability to either embark—or at least refuel helicopters.

During World War II—and the Falklands crisis—merchant ships were taken up from trade to augment the RFA fleet. Here the MFA (Merchant Fleet Auxiliary) *Aase Maersk* refuels a Colony Class Cruiser.

Ships of all sizes are customers of the RFA

Here, HMS Hermes takes on board fuel—for her own boilers and aviation fuel for her air group—from RFA Wave Baron. This operation could often take many hours for a carrier low on fuel.

..... Whilst a few minutes pumping by RFA Black Rover would fill the tanks of the tiny minehunter HMS Bildeston.

When not refuelling HM Ships RFA's need to adjust cargoes between themselves. Here RFA Tidesurge (centre) has her tanks filled by RFA's Wave Prince (left) and Wave Ruler (Oct 1961).

A different side to RFA life — beachead operations in the LSL's

Mexifloats, can be carried on the side of the LSL's and are lowered into the sea . . . . .

. . . . . Towed towards a beach . . . . .

Where embarked troops and equipment can be ferried ashore . . . . .

TO SAIL NO MORE . . .

Whilst most RFA's ended their days at a breakers yard—others didn't make it . . . . .

RFA Bacchus is sunk (Nov 1938) over the Hurd Deep.

Hemsley I (formerly RFA Scotol) off Trevose Head 1969.

RFA Green Ranger aground at Hartland 1962

RFA Ennerdale slips beneath the waves off the Seychelles. June 1970.

Index

144